Just Write

An easy-to-use guide to
writing at university

Bill Kirton and
Kathleen McMillan

Routledge
Taylor & Francis Group

LONDON AND NEW YORK

First published 2007
by Routledge
2 Park Square, Milton Park, Abingdon OX14 4RN

Simultaneously published in the USA and Canada
by Routledge
270 Madison Avenue, New York, NY 10016

*Routledge is an imprint of the Taylor & Francis Group,
an informa business*

© 2007 Bill Kirton and Kathleen McMillan

Typeset in Galliard and Gill Sans by
Florence Production Ltd, Stoodleigh, Devon
Printed and bound in Great Britain by
MPG Books Ltd, Bodmin, Cornwall

British Library Cataloguing in Publication Data
A catalogue record for this book is available from the British Library

Library of Congress Cataloging in Publication Data
A catalog record for this book has been applied for

ISBN10: 0–415–39677–8 (hbk)
ISBN10: 0–415–39678–6 (pbk)
ISBN10: 0–203–96585–X (ebk)

ISBN13: 978–0-415–39677–6 (hbk)
ISBN13: 978–0-415–39678–3 (pbk)
ISBN13: 978–0-203–96585–6 (ebk)

Contents

Acknowledgements

Our collaboration in this enterprise was made possible by the vision of the Royal Literary Fund. In order to help tackle the perceived problems of literacy in Higher Education, its members set up a scheme to place professional writers in universities and colleges throughout the UK as RLF Writing Fellows. The scheme has helped many students at all levels; it has also encouraged the writers themselves to analyze their craft from a different perspective and share their experiences with other Fellows. Special thanks are due to Steve Cook, the Fund's Fellowship and Education Officer, who matches writers with institutions and is tireless in his support of them all.

Introduction

Why do we need to write?

'She decided to run up a pair of trousers.'

Imagine the effect that such a sentence might have on someone learning English as a foreign language. They know the word 'run' and the word 'up' and so running up a hill or a flight of stairs makes perfect sense, but the idea of running up a garment must seem surrealistic. As must the fact that they can 'run across an old friend', 'run out of money' or 'feel run-down'. They're all examples of how language is flexible, creative but, equally, fragile in its relationship with meaning. In these examples, it's easy to avoid the difficulty by replacing 'run up' with 'make', 'run across' with 'meet', 'run out of' with 'have no more' and 'run-down' with 'unwell' but, if you're dealing with complex ideas, subtle distinctions and interpretations, it may be less straightforward. Nevertheless, for someone involved in academic studies, it's a skill that has to be acquired.

The first and most obvious thing to say about writing is that it's a way of communicating, but it's important to add that it's also what's being communicated. In other words, when you write something, you're not just creating a vehicle for your thoughts, you're creating the thoughts themselves. The very process of having to write out your ideas forces you to clarify and organize them. Think, for example, of 'morality' and 'racism'. Now put them together and work out a relationship between them. Whatever your ethnicity, or your political or other persuasions, the two notions – and the area between them in which you're bringing them together – are vague, spreading, unformed until you put actual words to them and pin them down. Either or both may provoke strong reactions in you but, until you have to articulate them, they're shapeless, subjective sensations. So writing helps you to think, to make sense of your experience. In the academic world, it's the way of confirming – to yourself and others – that you're understanding things.

It's generally accepted that, when it comes to writing assignments, most students find that the transition from secondary to higher education poses new challenges. In school, you were supplied with much of the material you needed and given guidelines to help you to handle and present it. At university, the onus is very much on you to define what you need, find it, and then organize it in a way that conforms to fairly strict academic conventions. At first, these conventions may seem artificial, overly rigid and inhibiting, but they're part of a wider educational process and, in the end, they work in your favour. Our aim in this book is simple. We want to demystify the notion of 'academic writing' and help you to develop your own techniques for researching and writing assignments by approaching them in a systematic way and reducing the major task to a sequence of smaller ones.

Sometimes, there's a feeling of artificiality about writing an academic assignment. The 'you' doing the writing seems different from the everyday 'you'. In addition to that, there's more than one 'you' involved – you have to be researcher, writer and editor. And the final part of this strange equation is the close relationship you must have with your reader. You're not writing in a vacuum, you're writing to be read.[1] You're trying to take your perhaps elusive personal thoughts and, by articulating them clearly and arranging them in particular sequences, make them accessible and comprehensible to a stranger. But that's where academic and linguistic conventions can help you. There's a collusion with the reader; she knows the rules within which you're working and you provide the signs and structures that help her to follow the path you've chosen. The formal writing conventions of academic style help you to convey a highly complex reality.

As we said, our aim is to help you to handle this complexity with confidence, but the first point to make is that we won't be providing templates for you to adapt or models for you to copy. Your writing style should develop from your own thinking and be suitable for your discipline and your particular institution. Indeed, if you adopted the same style that we'll be using throughout the book, you'd be fairly heavily penalized by most academic markers. Our aim here is to make a direct, person-to-person contact with you, so we'll be using terms and structures that are frankly conversational at times. Colloquialisms

---

1 This is one of many points you'll see reiterated throughout the book. The repetitions are deliberate and designed to reinforce our key messages.

such as 'OK' or contractions such as 'we'll' have no place in academic style, nor does the idea that there's a 'you' and 'us'. It tends to be formal, objective, neutral.

We're also going to be inventing our own conventions to make it easier for us to write and for you to read our text. You may have noticed, for example, that in our fourth paragraph we referred to the reader as 'she'. That's the way we're going to get round the problems associated with what's now known as 'gender neutral language'. Instead of writing 'he or she', 'him or her', 'his or her' every time we refer to an unidentified individual, we'll assume sometimes that it's a male and sometimes a female.[2]

Sometimes, we'll be using inverted commas around words to indicate that we're not intending them to be taken literally or that we're calling attention to their usage. For instance, we may identify 'correct', 'bad' or 'good' elements of a text, but the inverted commas will indicate that these are relative terms. You'll also find that we sometimes repeat ourselves, reprising a point in a different context. Once again, it's a deliberate strategy because we believe that constant reminders will help to reinforce the central points we're making.[3] Again, though, we don't recommend you copy it – repetition in the course of a short piece of work suggests a lack of sufficient original material.

As part of our intended 'reader-friendly' approach, we've tried to avoid 'technical' terminology wherever possible. Your interest is in using language effectively, not in knowing the linguistic labels that attach to its various features. Wherever possible, we've also avoided words that might be considered 'difficult'. However, you may still come across the occasional one that is unfamiliar so, if you do, look it up. An expanding vocabulary is fundamental to a wider education.

Our area of interest, as you know, is 'academic writing'. But even this simple expression needs to be defined. It may refer to anything from articles in journals to first-year essays, dissertations to PowerPoint presentations, doctoral theses to lecture notes. The strategies and techniques we'll be discussing could be adapted for all of these and many others so, to keep things simple, we've chosen to use the generic term 'assignments' to include all exercises that are written to be assessed.

Our intention in this introduction has been to make some general points about writing and give you an idea of what to expect. Many of

---

2 This issue is dealt with more fully in Chapter 7, where there's a section on inclusive and exclusive language.
3 See note 1 on p. 2.

the thoughts we've sketched here will be developed in the course of the book. The first chapter deals with how to get started, understand the assignment and identify the tools you have at your disposal. We then move on to discuss the nature of the specific task you're facing, how to break it down to make it easier to handle, and the departmental differences which may affect the way you approach it. We also stress the importance of organizing your time and making sure of the basic requirements.

Chapter 3 concentrates on developing reading strategies and collecting the material that's relevant to your topic and, in Chapter 4, we suggest how you can use the material itself to create the overall structure of the piece of work. Although we haven't yet mentioned any actual writing, all of this is central to the writing process, as you'll find in Chapter 5, which focuses on writing your first draft. The next two chapters consider style, conventions and how best to manipulate language not just to convey meaning but to give it impact. And last, but emphatically not least, comes a chapter devoted to editing, which we've deliberately separated from the actual writing.

In a way, the book has a narrative structure, trying to chart a course with you from the time you receive the instructions regarding the piece of work that's to be done through all its phases to final submission. It makes sense, therefore, to read it sequentially, rather than dip in and out of chapters, moving back and forth. But how you approach it is, of course, entirely your choice. We've included what we're calling 'Do-it-yourself' (DIY) sections to help you to practise some of the techniques being discussed. You'll find them at the end of each chapter. They're not the same as traditional 'exercises', which you complete before checking them against a 'correct' version. The DIY activities are included to help you identify, practise and adapt techniques to suit your particular needs. For most of them, there's no single 'correct' answer because they're not questions, they're ways of working.

At the end of the book, there's a section called 'Quick Reference' (QR). That's a list of some aspects of academic writing (and writing generally) that sometimes present problems for students. The intention is to give you a quick and easy way of identifying and overcoming any specific difficulties you may experience.

However you use the book, we hope that it'll not only help to take the stress out of writing assignments but also make you realize that writing doesn't have to be a chore; it can be a genuine pleasure.

Good luck.

Chapter 1

No problem

What am I doing here?

However competent and confident you are, universities and colleges can sometimes make you feel a bit uneasy. Fear may be too strong a word, but some of the experiences you have can provoke feelings of apprehension.

There's the impression that other students in tutorials contribute more than you do, seem more confident, more informed. Or the possibility that the marks you're getting for your essays aren't as good as they used to be at school. Some of the things you read and the lectures you hear are so full of unfamiliar words and complex structures that they almost sound like a foreign language. It's all too easy to start imagining that everyone else is sailing along effortlessly and that you're just . . . well . . . thick.

And, even if none of those comments applies to you, there's the newness of the experience, the unreality of it all. Perhaps for the first time, you're responsible for organizing your own timetables and work schedules, for having to look for answers and arguments rather than being shown them by a teacher. Depending on your chosen discipline, you're having to deal with abstractions, philosophy, engineering theory or any of the other demanding processes that seem to need a different level of understanding from the one you had at school. It can seem airy-fairy, irrelevant and, at times, you may wonder what any of it has to do with your everyday life. Well, in some ways, the answer is 'nothing'. Abstract or conceptual thinking doesn't get your teeth brushed or your stomach filled. It's an exercise.

But it's good for you. It may be hard for you to believe it at present, but it does help to improve your quality of life. You're exercising your mind, making it a better tool. And that's what we're trying to help you with here. This isn't a book for dummies; it's for anyone who wants to improve their written work and organize the way they think about things. Sometimes, thinking is hard, elusive, frustrating. And having to write down what you think is worse, because there's no hiding place. The words you choose commit you. You can go through life convinced that Shakespeare was a lousy writer, that Einstein had a poor grasp of physics and so on but, as soon as you say so or write down your opinion, it becomes a 'fact', which has to be proved and supported with evidence. So it obviously pays, in all walks of life, to be confident about how you use words.

Of course, people's problems or blind spots vary, so some of the things we say may seem obvious to you. It depends what you perceive your strengths and weaknesses to be. At this early stage, it might be useful for you to make a sort of checklist of issues you need to deal with. It may be that markers have written specific comments on a piece of your work saying that your sentences are too long or short, or that they're ambiguous. Perhaps the problems are with your choice of words, the overall structure or some deficiencies in critical analysis. And even if you've had no such comments, you may feel that you know of some specific problems you need to tackle. Take some time to think about your writing and ask yourself where, if anywhere, you need help. The first DIY task at the end of the chapter will help you to focus your analysis.

DIY

Evaluate your own writing skills

Academic writing

DIY

What is academic writing?

The first thing to address is academic writing itself. You'll be using and seeing many different types and we'll deal with them a little later in this chapter but, for now, let's look at the sort of thing that often seems as incomprehensible as Klingon.

One of the early experiences at university that sometimes contributes to feelings of inadequacy is that of reading academic books and articles. Here's a quotation to show you what we mean. The first few words will probably be enough to depress you, but read it anyway. There's a good reason for it, you'll see.

Given the Hegelian preference for meso-morphic declinations of syntactical variables, dysfunctional paradigms of primordial reces-sion are endemic in any coherent lexis of digressive para-linguistic modalities. Thus, semiological interpretation of intertextual anomalies necessarily engenders a phenomenological disassociation which is, in its constituent elements, complete rubbish.

The last two words sum it up. It's not a quotation from any learned article, it's something we just made up. It's an example of the worst type of academic writing, writing that calls attention to its own importance. It uses long, impressive words and complicated constructions, but it says nothing. Writing that fails to communicate is bad writing. So, don't worry; not only do you not have to write that sort of thing, it's counter-productive to try to do so.

DIY

The nonsense generator

Getting started

The suggestions we're going to make can be applied to all sorts of writing – academic, commercial, journalistic, even creative (although we'd maintain that almost all forms of writing are in some way creative) – but, to keep things simple, we'll focus on the sort that's required for exercises such as projects, case studies, reports and, of course, essays. And, as we said earlier, to avoid boring or confusing you by repeating that little list every few sentences, we'll use the word 'assignment' as a general term that covers all of them.

First, let's make sure we understand the other terms we'll be using. Students often talk about having to do an essay QUESTION and that's misleading. If there's a question, that presupposes that there's an answer. It also implies that the answer could be right or wrong. Of course, an essay title can take the form of a question – for example, 'What effect did the USA's economic policies have on the development of post-war Europe?' – but, perhaps more frequently, it's phrased as an instruction, as we'll see in the five examples we'll look at next. So, rather than think of an essay as a question that calls for an answer, think of it as an instruction that needs a response. And don't think in terms of right and wrong.

QR

Instruction words

The good thing about essays is that they give you both the recipe and the ingredients for what you're going to make – in other words, a title. It tells you the topic you have to deal with, the particular aspects of it to concentrate on and the approach to take to organizing them. The sort of essay topics you'll get will obviously depend on your chosen discipline. We've tried to invent generalized essay titles that, in terms of what they're asking for, should be accessible to students in all disciplines. Some examples will show what we mean:

- Account for the rise in unemployment in the inter-war period in Britain and the USA.
- Discuss the presumed trends in flower structure during the evolution of the angiosperms.
- Evaluate different methods of energy production adopted in the UK since 1945.
- Compare the structure and life cycles of red algae with those of brown algae.
- 'In *Madame Bovary*, the narrative is driven by emotions rather than events.' Discuss.

You don't need to know anything about the subjects to recognize that each title is made up of the same elements. There's a word or expression to tell you what approach to take. That's the instruction:

- Account for
- Discuss (twice)
- Evaluate
- Compare.

There's the main topic:

- unemployment
- flower structure
- energy production
- red algae
- the narrative in *Madame Bovary*.

There's an indication of which aspect or aspects of the topic you should concentrate on:

- the rise in (unemployment)
- the presumed trends in (flower structure)
- different methods of (energy production)
- the structure and life cycles of (red algae)
- (the narrative is) driven by.

And finally, there are elements (one or more), that restrict your study:

- in the inter-war period (1), in Britain (2), and in the USA (3)
- during the evolution of angiosperms
- adopted in the UK (1) since 1945 (2)
- with those of brown algae
- emotions (1) rather than events (2).

Breaking it down

So, the first thing to do when you're given an essay title is decide exactly what it's asking for. If there are any words or expressions in it you're not sure about, look them up, ask about them, do something to make sure that you're not missing the point or misinterpreting some part of the title. Then ask yourself, what's the topic? Are there any specific aspects of it to concentrate on? Are there any restrictions that limit the field of study? And what are you being instructed to do – compare, discuss, describe, or something else? If it helps, jot down the answers to your questions in your own words. Understanding exactly what's required of you is a sound basis for a good essay. You'll find some sample essay titles from a variety of subjects at the end of the chapter. Use them to practise your 'breaking down' technique.

You know, then, what's expected of you. Breaking the title down into its component parts helps you to focus clearly on your area of enquiry, so you know what sort of material you need to collect. If you're writing the first of our five sample essays, for instance, you can see that statistics about French unemployment, or unemployment in Britain in 1945 are irrelevant (unless, of course, you're using them to make a point about unemployment in inter-war Britain).

A little warning: avoid the tendency to jump to conclusions or to write a partial response. Sometimes students do concentrate on just one facet of a topic because they know a lot about that part of it. In other words, they answer a question that isn't being asked. When faced with the title 'Discuss the importance of Lady Macbeth in her husband's decision-making processes', it might be tempting to concentrate on writing a detailed character study of Lady Macbeth. The title is, after all, implying that she's important. But the topic is Macbeth's 'decision-making processes' and there may be many other influences on them. Lady Macbeth will obviously figure largely in the essay, but it's not exclusively about her.

In your essay, be sure to deal with all the required elements.

First steps

OK, you know what you're looking for. What next? Well, you're going to have to argue for or against a case (or maybe both, if the instruction involves comparison or contrast), and that means you'll need some substance to back up the points you make. In other words, you need the ingredients for your essay.

Where you get them will depend on a variety of things. In the sciences, for example, you may need to conduct experiments and produce or refer to graphs, charts or tables. In the social sciences, there may be questionnaires to analyze or interviews to organize. We can't anticipate every eventuality but we can identify some of the basics.

Getting started is rarely easy. What if, having tried what we've just suggested, you're still finding that the question's phrased in 'difficult' terms or that its meaning still seems elusive? Well, there are some common strategies that may help.

First, just try to rephrase the question in simpler terms. Use your own words instead of those in the original, write down your version and compare the two. Also, jot down quickly what you already know about the topic – not in any structured way, just as quick notes, bits of shorthand to start building the heap of material you'll need. Do some brainstorming. Look at what you've written down and see where else it leads you, follow any associations and jot them down, too. You may discard some or all of them later but, for now, just let your mind wander round the subject and look at it from different angles.

DIY

Sample essay questions

An important part of writing (and learning in general) is asking questions. Ask yourself, ask other people. The answers you get or give will open up more possibilities, stimulate more questions. At the moment, all you're doing is collecting material. You're not trying to see where it fits or even if it's any use; the important thing is that you're finding something to say. What it is and how you'll say it will come later.

If you can't think of any appropriate questions, use the basic technique of asking yourself who? what? which? when? where? why? and how?

- Who's it for? Who has an opinion on this topic? Who's affected by it?
- What's the instruction word? What's the main point? What do I need? What opinion is being expressed in the title (if any)?
- Which words or expressions are important? Which sources will give me the information I need?

- When's the deadline? When should I stop researching and start writing?
- Where is the title leading? Where can I find the information I need?
- Why is the title being phrased in this particular way? Why are particular words preferred to others?
- How can I break it down into manageable segments? How should I organize the material?

These are just quick examples; you'll find that more and different ones are prompted by different essay titles. It's just a way of getting your brain started on the topic.

If you want, you can refine this collecting process by making spider diagrams or idea clusters. It's the same process as brainstorming, but as you jot down your ideas, you start creating a structure by linking them with one another so that you can see how they relate to the main topic or to an aspect of it or to one of the question's restrictions.

> **QR**
> Spider diagrams, idea clusters, brainstorming

A variation on spider diagrams is to use Post-its®. By writing your ideas, references and quotations on them, it's easy to move them around to see how best they fit together. You could maybe stick them on the wall over your desk or table where they're easy to see. That way, you can check your layout, see whether it's sound and think about how you could improve it.

Whichever technique you use, it'll give you the beginnings of your essay. By looking at what you've written, you'll see where your strengths are and, perhaps more important, where there are gaps that you need to fill. Maybe the gaps outnumber the strengths. Maybe the whole thing is still just one huge gap. Don't worry, the next phase will correct that. It's time to do some research.

What tools are available?

Whatever your subject, there's far more information available than you'll ever need. Your own ideas are important and valuable, but you can add to or develop them by using lecture notes, books, articles, the Internet, discussions with tutors and fellow students, even radio and television programmes. You'll know better than we do what's available in your particular discipline at your particular institution, but there's one technique that you could use to make things easier for yourself later. It works like this.

QR

Note-making
and note-
taking

Most people, when they're reading books or articles or a piece on the Internet, make notes as they go along. Sometimes, it's easier to photocopy an article or a few pages and highlight the sections and ideas that interest you. But whether you use these techniques or any others, you end up with several pages of notes. And, when you're writing the essay, it takes time to sift through them to find the reference you're looking for. That's fine, and it refreshes your overall grasp of the subject, but it can take ages and it can interrupt the flow of your thinking. You may find the reference at last, then have to remind yourself why you wanted it and how it fits in.

It's a question of time management. You've got a deadline to meet and you want to waste as little time as possible, so if there's a way of speeding up the reference-finding process, you should use it. Our suggestion is, first, that you should try to use a note-making method that'll make it easier to find your way around them. That's why we've included a Quick Reference on various methods of note-making and note-taking.[1] The second part of our suggestion is that, having made it easier to locate the relevant notes, quotations and pieces of information, when you're selecting them for an assignment, you transfer them to individual pieces of card or paper. You could achieve the same effect and save some time by using your normal notepad but only writing on one side. Then, when you need to isolate a particular piece of information, you can just cut it out and set it aside. This is already easy to achieve with highlighted extracts from photocopies. At this point, it may seem a quirky, perhaps puzzling thing to do but when we come to structuring the essay, you'll see how useful it is.

Write clearly

There's a certain mystique about academic writing. The ability to produce it seems to let you into a secret society, all of whose members are intellectually superior to ordinary mortals. It's the product of a process of rigorous analysis, carefully chosen words, all designed to explore and explain our experience of the world. And it's central to our culture.

But . . .

---

1 See pp. 140–6.

As we saw earlier, it's sometimes stifled by its own cleverness. So, don't let the mystique cloud your vision. Academic writing takes many forms; at its best, it gives us real insights and affects the way we perceive things; at its worst, it's self-congratulatory and irrelevant. If you gather your material carefully, organize it to support your arguments and present your findings clearly, you'll be a legitimate member of the 'at its best' club.

Of course, you won't just be writing essays or dissertations. You'll need to develop techniques for the other sorts of writing that are required, such as making notes, giving presentations in tutorials and seminars, summarizing other people's arguments. In each case, though, the need is the same – what you write must be as clear as you can make it. Always remember that you're writing to be read.

QR

Difference between spoken and written language

There is, of course, a difference between writing to be heard and writing to be read, between spoken and written language. With spoken language, rules are less strictly applied. You can get away with expressions such as 'get away with'; you can contract expressions and say 'don't', 'can't', 'isn't'. As we said in the introduction, the style we're using in this book is deliberately conversational and shouldn't be adopted in any academic exercise that is to be submitted for assessment.

Academic disciplines have their own terminology, which often relies necessarily on 'long' words.[2] They may not actually be difficult but they may seem so because they don't occur all that frequently in everyday usage. You'll find that, as you study your particular subjects, these words will become more familiar and you'll feel much more comfortable about using them. But good writing always makes its meaning clear. So don't make the mistake of thinking you have to write in some special convoluted way in order to play the academic game.[3] If the choice is between an impressive-sounding word whose meaning you're not absolutely sure of and a simpler word about which you're confident, go for simplicity every time. We're not suggesting that you content yourself with 'The cat sat on the mat' or '2B or not 2B', just that you should always keep your reader in mind. You want to be understood. So write clearly.

DIY

Spoken and written language

---

2 These 'long' words are often not long but unusual and it is students' unfamiliarity with such words that makes them difficult.
3 If you don't know what 'convoluted' means, make a note of it now and look it up later.

So, where are we now?

You've written nothing yet, but you've begun to organize your thinking about the essay. You know that you understand the question, you've identified the areas you need to focus on, and you know that the information you need is accessible. After all the brainstorming and questions, you may realize that, already, you know more than you thought you did. Your opinion is valid, worthwhile, so don't be afraid to develop your own voice.

Which means what exactly? Well, it doesn't mean writing 'I think' or 'In my opinion' or using similar expressions. You're not writing an opinion, you're presenting an argument, supported by evidence.

But the way in which you choose to present it is particular to you. You're choosing the content and organizing it; you're deciding which words to use and the sequences in which you put them – that's your voice. So don't try to write something that seems artificial to you; use words and sentence structures you're comfortable with. But be aware of register. That's another word for style. We'll deal with the topic in more detail in Chapter 5 but, for the moment, remember that you're not jotting down a quick note for your friends, so don't resort to the words and techniques you use for texting or emails. And don't copy the conversational style we're using in this book either.

DIY

Avoiding personalized language

One step at a time

Earlier, we referred to time management. Life is short; you don't want to waste time, so managing your schedules efficiently isn't just a good way of dealing with an assignment, it's also good training for a future career as well as for organizing your life generally.

So, when you're handed an essay title and told that it has to be in by a particular date, if your reaction is to start worrying about it, putting it off, finding other pressing things that need to be done, you're making things worse. You're wasting time and nervous energy on feelings that are negative and counter-productive. The FACT is that it has to be done by a given date. The REALITY is that you'll have to spend some of that time doing it. So organize things so that it occupies just the necessary part of that time, and you're not ALWAYS thinking about it. If you keep putting it off, it's harder and harder to get started and the whole exercise looms large in the future like some malevolent enemy.

Don't think of it as 'writing an assignment', think of it as performing a sequence of separate tasks – thinking, research, analysis, organization, writing, editing.[4] Some people can just sit down and write an essay and it may be fine, but most of us can't. There's a better chance of it having some substance and being more persuasive if it's been properly researched, if you consider what others have said about the subject and about what changes in attitude there have been on the topic. We're convinced that all writing benefits from some serious, considered editing. If you think something through yourself first and understand it, there's a better chance that the reader will understand it, too. A considered response is always likely to be more reasonable and effective than a knee-jerk reaction.

One final thought before we move on: this book isn't THE way to write an essay; it's A way. It doesn't prescribe a 'one-fits-all' remedy; it gives you options. It's up to you to decide which working method suits you best. You may prefer to edit after you've written just a few pages or to wait until you've completed the whole essay. You may feel more comfortable creating a plan before you start anything else. The important thing is to work with a system that suits you. Whatever the exercise – essay, report, presentation, or some other document – it's an expression of your thinking, articulated in your own voice, and the manner in which you create and produce it is as personal as your opinion. So we're not setting down any rules here; we're just trying to smooth the path. But, whatever technique you use, make sure the product you hand in is as good as you can make it.

---

4 This is dealt with more fully in the next chapter. See figure, p. 30.

DIY TASK 1

Evaluate your own writing skills

The following questions are designed to help you to start thinking about yourself as a writer. Be honest in your evaluation about how you rate yourself.

Preparation	Yes	No
1 Do you routinely read the course handbook for general writing guidelines?	☐	☐
2 Do you routinely consult the handbook for guidance on presentation?	☐	☐
3 Do you routinely consult the handbook for guidance on grammar?	☐	☐
4 Do you follow the subject-specific guidance given in the course handbook?	☐	☐
5 Do you establish what the learning outcomes are for the task before you start?	☐	☐
6 Do you identify the mark allocation for the task as part of the overall assessment?	☐	☐

Planning		
7 Do you analyse the task you've been set to identify what's expected of you?	☐	☐
8 Do you plan the task ahead stage by stage?	☐	☐
9 Do you plan out the time that you can allocate to each of the stages?	☐	☐

Writing		
10 Do you write a first draft and then edit it?	☐	☐
11 Do you begin by writing the main body?	☐	☐
12 Do you write sentences that are well-balanced?	☐	☐
13 Do you write sentences that are unambiguous?	☐	☐
14 Do you write paragraphs that are well-balanced?	☐	☐
15 Do you write paragraphs that flow easily from one to the other?	☐	☐
16 Do you write paragraphs?	☐	☐
17 Is it easy for you to find words that express your meaning?	☐	☐
18 Is it easy for you to write in the formal manner required in academic contexts?	☐	☐

Editing		
19 Do you routinely spell-check your work?	☐	☐
20 Do you routinely grammar-check your work?	☐	☐
21 Do you always keep a back-up copy of your writing?	☐	☐

Feedback		
22 Does feedback on your writing suggest that you are an expert writer?	☐	☐
23 Do your marks reflect the effort that you put into writing the text?	☐	☐
24 Do you feel confident about how you write?	☐	☐
25 Do you have opportunities to share your writing concerns with others?	☐	☐

DIY TASK 2

What is academic writing?

As we've seen in this chapter, academic writing isn't confined simply to writing academic essays or reports. It'll also vary according to the way you, as an individual, approach it, what subjects you're studying, and several other factors. That's why we've included this DIY task at this early stage. We've listed some typical academic writing activities. First of all, look through them and add any others that you think are particular to you, your subject and your learning activities. Note how frequently you're required to use each sort of writing and whether it has to be formal or informal.

	Never ←——→ Often	Formal	Informal
Accident reports			
Application forms			
Risk assessment reports			
Curriculum vitae			
Diary for professional activity			
Essay			
Lab notebook			
Lab reports			
Labelling work			
Letter-writing			
Note-making			
Note-taking			
Posters			
PowerPoint or other oral presentation			
Progress notes			
Questionnaires/Surveys			
Writing a brief			
Visa application supporting letter			

Now, based on this appraisal, define academic writing by completing the following sentence.

Academic writing should be _____

_____

_____

Finally, come back to this task again when you've finished reading this book and decide whether you want to change what you think academic writing means.

DIY TASK 3

The nonsense generator

The idea here is to show how easy it is to cobble together expressions that give a false impression of intellectual control. So think of any random sequence of six numbers from 0 to 9, then use them to choose words from columns A, B and C in sequence to insert into the following sentence:

> Studies have shown conclusively that (A) (B) (C) lead inexorably to the paradox of (A) (B) (C).

For example, if you chose 0, 1, 2 for the first sequence and 3, 4, 5 for the second sequence, your sentence would read:

> Studies have shown conclusively that intuitively deconstructive morphologies lead inexorably to the paradox of indecipherable polymorphic structures.

Whichever sequence you choose, you'll produce results that will sound impressive but mean nothing.

	A	B	C
0	intuitively	interdependent	anomalies
1	complementary	deconstructive	paradigms
2	fundamentally	disparate	morphologies
3	indecipherable	internalized	data sets
4	pathologically	polymorphic	meta-analyses
5	intransigent	politicized	structures
6	exponentially	volatile	periphrases
7	ethically	post-modern	values
8	pharmaceutically	inert	variables
9	metaphysically	dysfunctional	dichotomies

DIY TASK 4

Sample essay questions

There's not room here to represent every single subject taught at universities, of course, but we've tried to create sample questions to cover a range of different disciplines. Even if your particular specialization isn't here, it will still be useful (and interesting) for you to practise breaking them down into their component parts. Seeking out the central topics, aspects and restrictions of titles in areas where you have no (or little) expertise will sharpen your general comprehension of what's required. And, anyway, you don't have to write the essays, so what have you got to lose?

Medicine/epidemiology

Type of disability	1981		1991	
	number	%	number	%
Locomotor	5427	39.68	8044	49.16
Visual	3474	25.41	3626	22.16
Hearing	3019	22.08	2924	17.97
Speech	1754	12.83	1768	10.81
Total	13674	100.00	16362	100.00

- This table shows numerically the estimated extent of disabilities in India for the period 1981 and 1991. Compare and contrast the details in general and for each category in particular.

Sociology
- Identify the role of public services in the support of the weak in society.
- 'Poverty is a local rather than a global issue.' Discuss with special reference to Africa and the USA.

Philosophy
- Is it legitimate for the State to prevent one from doing harm to oneself?
- Examine Descartes' ontological assertion: 'I think. Therefore, I am.'
- Compare and contrast the ethics of euthanasia.

Economics
- Give a broad definition of the term 'inflation' and explain the concepts of anticipated and unanticipated inflation.

English
- To what extent could it be said that Dickens' *A Christmas Carol* was a commentary on social, political and economic life in Britain in the nineteenth century?
- 'The character of the eponymous hero in *Jude the Obscure* is designed to confirm the negativity of life rather than provide insights into the human mind.' Discuss.
- With reference to any two of Shakespeare's plays, examine the assertion that intellect is an insignificant factor in our response to tragedy.

History
- Assess the roles of Mazzini, Garibaldi and Cavour in the unification of Italy.
- Critically analyse the nature of international treaties from the Congress of Vienna to the Treaty of Versailles.

Politics
- Consider the view that a federation of European states is an economic disaster waiting to happen.
- Explain how an individual British citizen can call political representatives to account.

Biology
- Identify the factors that contribute to plant growth and evaluate their relative importance at each phase of the growth cycle.
- Using specific examples, describe and account for the differences between plant and animal cells.

DIY TASK 5

Spoken and written language

Here are some examples of comparisons between spoken and written language. The passages in the left-hand column use colloquialisms and are less clearly structured than those opposite them. The point is not that one's 'better' than the other; each is appropriate to its context. So note the differences between the two and try to keep the looseness of speech out of your writing.

Spoken	Written
We got the stuff together and tried it out, to see whether it was the right gear. Some of the ones we got from France were a bit dodgy so we went for the German ones. They were OK, but they still didn't do the trick. No doubt about it, the American ones were way ahead. Maybe they were older, maybe it's because they're more of an American thing. Whatever the reason, they're the ones that got everybody's yes vote.	The material was collected and tested to establish its validity. Some of the French samples were of poor quality so preference was given to those from Germany, which were of a higher standard but still failed to achieve the desired result. There was little doubt that the American items were superior. The difference may have derived from the fact that they were older, or that they are more naturally associated with American culture but, whatever the reason, they were the ones that received universal approval.
Science always wants to make sure things that seem real are real. If you're a scientist and you're doing an experiment that comes up with some weird results, you've got to do it again to show that it's not a fluke. Maybe you were tired and missed something. You might have messed up the figures, got things the wrong way round, or even, if you were trying to con people, deliberately faked your results.	Science always seeks to distinguish between appearance and reality. If a scientific experiment produces anomalous results, it must be repeated to confirm its validity. Many factors might have influenced the outcomes: fatigue, a miscalculation, a faulty technique. The results might even have been distorted in a deliberate attempt to mislead.

Here are some more for you to practise on. There's no single way of reshaping them and, even if you only try parts of them it'll help you to recognize the differences and exercise better control over your own writing style:

- Sport's supposed to be good for you – cardio-vascular workouts, calorie burns, hand–eye co-ordination, stuff like that. But we don't seem to bother much about exercising our minds. Surely that's just as important because we're not just machines, are we? There's a person in there somewhere – somebody who's special, not like anybody else.

- The trouble with extra sensory perception is you can't prove it. You hear all sorts of creepy stories about things disappearing, ghosts with no heads, music playing in empty rooms – but where are the recordings, the photos, or anything to prove it? Most of the time, people come out with all this rubbish because they want you to take notice of them, or maybe they've had one too many. There's enough craziness in the world already without inventing more.

- The first lot of plants were supposed to show what happened when you gave them half as much light as they needed, which would have been fine if one of the guys in the group hadn't set the timer all wrong. Result? They get a full twenty-four hours of bright sunlight and when we go to check them out, they're sticking out the top of the box like bamboo shoots.

You could also create some examples of your own. Try picking a topic related to your studies and jotting down the sort of remarks you might make about it in conversation, then rewrite them in the way you would if you were using them in an essay.

DIY TASK 6

Avoiding personalized language

The idea of this task is to focus specifically on rearranging words in order to avoid using 'I', 'we' and other pronouns that personalize your work and make it seem less objective and, therefore, less 'academic'. First, some examples:

Original version	Revised version
After collating the results, we divided them into categories by determining their perceived importance in the eyes of our respondents.	The collated results were divided into categories by determining their perceived importance in the eyes of the respondents.
I have based my conclusions on the notes I made as I observed how the foster parents interacted with the child.	The report's conclusions were based on observations made of the interactions between the foster parents and the child.
I intend to show that the multinational companies involved in exploration operations in the delta failed to prioritize their environmental agenda.	This study proposes to investigate the degree of priority the multinational companies involved in exploration operations gave to the environmental agenda.[5]
We think that, as long as current trends continue to demonstrate volatility, the economic variables will favour the maintenance of the status quo.	As long as current trends continue to demonstrate volatility, the economic variables will favour the maintenance of the status quo.
The main problems arise when you have to choose between applying a traditional Marxist historical analysis and one of its more recent variations.	The main problems arise when a choice has to be made between applying a traditional Marxist historical analysis and one of its more recent variations.
It was important to validate one's research findings to ensure that one's own prejudices did not unduly influence the eventual conclusions.	It was important to validate the findings to ensure that the researcher's own prejudices did not influence the conclusions.[6]

5 Notice how, in this example, we haven't just eliminated the pronoun, we've also got rid of the value judgement and pre-emptive conclusions implied in the words 'show' and 'failed to'. You'll find a fuller reference to value judgements in Chapter 7.

6 Note also here how removing the words 'unduly' and 'eventual' improve the sentence. They add nothing to the meaning and, especially in the case of 'unduly', they betray the presence of someone who's making judgements. Subjectivity isn't confined to words such as 'I' and 'we'.

Now here are some for you to try for yourself. Remember, there's no single 'correct' way to rewrite them, so see if you can find different versions for each:

- To test our thesis, we will expose polyatomic molecules to light and note how much fragmentation we see and what products we get from it.

- In my opinion, it is the exchange of energy and angular momentum that determines the decay pathways of the whole process.

- In order to prepare our subjects for testing, we measured the electrical signals produced by the sensory neurones and compared them with the statistics we'd been given on relay and motor neurones.

- It seems obvious to me that Dickens created his villains to give shape to the social forces that were corrupting society and to give us easy insights into its overall morality.

- I based this design on materials I collected in the course of a recent field trip. I arranged them into categories, chose those in the middle of the spectrum and combined them with my chosen medium to eliminate the contrasts I'd seen in the first print.

- As architects, the targets we set ourselves vary according to the type of building and the people who'll live or work in it. We therefore tend to classify a structure according to use because this also tells us what sort of people will be in it. Thus, whether I'm religious or not, if I'm asked to design a church, I'll have a pretty good idea of how to allocate space to highlight the main symbols and images of the faith involved.

Chapter 2

What's it all about?

What next?

In order to do yourself justice, you should think beyond the title of the assignment. In the last chapter, we spent all our time unpicking it, making sure we knew what was being asked and defining the terms clearly for ourselves. That's obviously important, because if you don't know what it's supposed to be about, how can you write it? But you also need to think of other things. Who's it for? Who's going to be reading it? How much information is available? What balance should there be between your own ideas and the opinions of the experts you may be quoting from?

And what about style? It's hard to imagine that your tutors will be impressed if, for example, they've asked you to write about the influence of Vedic and Buddhist teachings on the philosophy of Schopenhauer and you hand in a script that begins 'Schopenhauer is cool'. If you've taken the advice we gave you before, you'll either have (or know how to get) enough material to construct an argument, but its effect on the reader will depend on HOW you present it. And that's style. You're having to choose your words, avoid ambiguity, wrap your ideas up in a way that makes them easily accessible to the person reading your work. You may have a passionate belief about some aspect of your subject, but passion is often difficult to articulate. Turning it into words will force you to look at it more carefully, understand where the passion comes from, see just how complex it is. And if you don't have such a passion, the act of putting words together to describe or analyse something will, once again, help you to see it in a different light and maybe even generate something like passion for it. Whatever your starting point, by forcing yourself to find the right form of words, the right combinations of sentences and paragraphs, you'll actually make ideas clearer for yourself (and, of course, for the reader).

First reference point – your tutor

In his play *Huis clos,* Sartre wrote that 'Hell is other people'. And it's easy for some students to imagine that, when he said it, he was thinking of his tutor. There they are, these students, having a good time, and there's this person who keeps setting them assignments, making them think, spoiling their fun. But for every student who thinks that way, there are many others who know that the tutor's their first point of contact with the dreaded 'system'. They guide you through your course, teaching you and helping you to teach yourself. They know the work that you've done (or that you're supposed to have done), and the pieces of work they set are designed both to check how well you're understanding it and to encourage you to involve yourself in it more closely.

And remember, too, that they've been there and done that. In other words, they were at your stage once, maybe complaining about their tutors, certainly being faced with the task of gathering information and writing essays, so they do understand what you're going through and know the sort of problems you're facing.

So, if there's anything you don't understand about an assignment – whether it's the content, the way in which it should be presented, or any other aspect of the exercise, the logical thing to do is consult your tutor. But, before you rush off to his or her room, think about it. Are you really stuck? Have you really tried to sort out the difficulty yourself? Tutors are very busy people; they've got lots of other students to help, classes to prepare, their own books and articles to write and, in today's universities, meetings to go to and administrative duties to take care of. Make sure that you're not wasting their time. If you arrive at their door and just say 'I don't understand this title', we think a legitimate answer might be 'Well, go away and think about it'. But it's an answer that'll just deepen your gloom.

So the first thing to do is check any guidance literature that you were given, such as your course module or departmental handbook, or notes and instructions on virtual learning environments. They'll give you advice on how to do things and the notes on your module will probably list the learning outcomes they're designed to achieve. Just check them to make sure you haven't missed something. Use them and anything else to work out exactly what it is you need help with. Is it some part of the wording? Does it seem ambiguous? Are there unfamiliar expressions or concepts involved? Or do you simply need reassurance that you've interpreted the title correctly?

After all that, if you're still stuck and the thing you have to say to your tutor really is 'I don't understand this title', you can at least show that you truly have tried to work it out for yourself. Let him know how you've approached the title, the questions you've asked yourself about it, the things you've looked up in the dictionary. You'll get a much better reception if it's obvious that you've already been working at it, thinking about it and taking the task seriously. You never know, the very fact of identifying exactly where the problem lies may help you to solve it for yourself.

Departmental differences

We said in Chapter 1 that this isn't THE way to write an assignment, it's A way. Even if we did have some magic formula that everyone could apply to their writing, it would still have to acknowledge that the term 'essay' (or 'report', or 'case study' or whatever other assignment you've been set) can mean different things to different people and that, at university, individuals and departments may interpret it in a variety of ways. For the moment, let's focus on essays. Before you start working on one, it makes sense to find out what your particular department understands by the term, what's encouraged and what's unacceptable. You may think that presenting some data or a sequence of arguments as bullet points makes them clearer but, if your department thinks bullet points and essays don't mix, you've got a problem. You'll notice that, in this book, we're using sub-headings. The idea of that is to break the text up into easily identifiable aspects of the subject, so that you always know where you are. If this were an essay, many departments would probably mark us down for that. Some, though, wouldn't. So, make sure that you know what sort of essay conventions your department prefers.

DIY

Using sub-headings

Cross-disciplinary concerns

There's also the fact that different disciplines call for different approaches to the substance of the essay and the way it's observed, organized and reported. For a long time, for example, science and engineering students have worked with a familiar template. Broadly speaking, it works like this:

- *Introduction.* (To tell the reader what you're going to be doing and what the terms of reference are. This is also a chance to outline how you're interpreting the subject.)
- *Literature review.* (A selective survey of what others have written and/or said about the subject.)

- *Methodology.* (The methods you'll be using in the course of the study, for example, analysis of data, collation of observations or comparison of results.)
- *Argument.* (The body of the work, which may involve different approaches. You might, for example, present your evidence and indicate its significance, or perhaps report your results, discuss them and draw relevant conclusions.)
- *Conclusion.* (A summary of your overall approach and findings and of what you think you have proved.)

It's a well-tried system and it's been used by many non-scientific disciplines, too. If we reduce it to basics, you can see that it ticks all the necessary boxes. You're introducing the subject, saying what you've read about it, telling the reader what approach you'll be taking, leading her through your argument, and drawing your conclusions. It's obviously suited to exercises where the description or analysis of data is important, and less useful when you're being asked to speculate about the theme of regeneration in *King Lear.*

At this point we're having to generalize more than we'd like to, but there isn't space to do justice to each academic discipline. What we say here about the differences between the sciences and the humanities in terms of academic writing should only be read as broad guidelines to suggest what may be expected of you. As ever, the best way to proceed is to find out what's approved of and what's prohibited by your department. But, to continue with our generalizations, it seems legitimate to say that science essays are more concerned with facts. You may be asked to describe observations you've made – of experiments or processes – or to compare or classify things. You may need to write up results, analyse statistics, prove or apply mathematical formulae or equations. The subject may be a specific experiment, in which case you'd be expected to tell the reader what it was for, how you did it, what results you got and what those results mean. All in all, the stress is on reporting facts objectively.

Essays in the humanities have a different emphasis. It's a difference expressed (perhaps a bit too forcefully) by the eighteenth-century philosopher, Jean-Jacques Rousseau. Very near the beginning of his *Discourse on the Origin of Inequality,* he wrote: 'So, let's begin by setting aside all the facts, because they've got nothing to do with the question.' He went on to say that research findings aren't historical truths but relative, hypothetical arguments. We wouldn't put it quite as strongly as that, but you can appreciate that investigating the causes of the French

Revolution, identifying and evaluating a particular type of imagery in a novel, play or poem, or simply answering the philosophical question 'Why is this question difficult to answer?' all call for something other than factual observation. A more accurate term might be 'informed speculation'.

But what does this mean for you? If you're a scientist dealing with facts, does that mean you need to be more precise when selecting your words? If you're a student of language, literature or history, can you get away with looser constructions and terms that are only approximate? Well, the answer's obvious – choosing your words with precision and presenting your arguments in a clear, rigorous way is critical, whether you're writing about sub-atomic particles or 'Ode to a Nightingale'.

So, for scientists and for students in the humanities, the tools and terminology may be different, but the exercise is the same. Choose your words carefully, and organize your own ideas and your supporting material in such a way that you present the reader with a clear, consistent argument.

Word count

The sort of differences we're talking about can fall under various headings, such as style, academic conventions, layout, length, and flexibility with regard to deadlines. Let's start with a relatively straightforward one: how long should the assignment be? You might be surprised at how widely the answer to this question can vary. Sometimes, there may not even be a limit either way; you may be told that it should be 'as long as it needs to be' – not a very helpful piece of advice, but a legitimate comment if you accept that you're responsible for making your own choices and decisions and articulating them to the best of your ability. So, find out whether the essay is expected to be of a particular length (in terms of words or pages) and, if it is, try not to be too far either side of it.[1]

But don't worry too much about it until you've reached the final stages of the exercise. If you're approaching the essay as if it's a container that has to be filled with, say, 2,000 words, your focus is on quantity instead of quality. After all, it's not just any old 2,000 words you want, it's words that are relevant, well organized, meaningful.

---

1 Remember that font and point size, margins, line-spacing, diagrams, tables, headers and footers will all make a difference to your page count.

Another effect of being too aware of your word count is that the essay can become unbalanced. If you start writing and keep checking how much you've written as you go along, you'll get a false reading. The impulse will be to think: 'Oh, not many words yet. Better put in a few more here.' So the earlier part of the work gets filled out. Then, as you near the end, you realize that you're going to reach the target so there's no need to keep adding things. Result? The latter part is under-written.

One final point: cutting words out almost always produces a better result than adding them.[2] As a general rule, your strategy should be to write more rather than less, then work through it and delete what's less necessary (or sometimes, you'll find, unnecessary). Most writers agree that every type of writing benefits from being cut. The opposite approach, in which students find that they haven't written enough and have to pad the material out, produces an obviously uneven effect. It's like stuffing a cushion or pillow: you fill it so that its texture's even and it feels comfortable, then you add bits to make it bigger and, suddenly, it's lumpy. It's still, potentially, a very nice cushion but all you notice are the lumps.

DIY

The naked sentence

Word count is important. It shows that you can discipline yourself to say what you have to say within the set limits. But it should never be allowed to dictate how you write.

Timescale

This may seem too obvious to be worth including but, again, you need to know not only when the essay has to be handed in but also whether there's any flexibility built into the system. Some departments may have a more relaxed attitude to deadlines; others, perhaps for administrative purposes, may be required to apply them more strictly. Imagine how you'd feel if you'd put a lot of time and effort into an exercise, then handed it in too late for it to be marked. And if you think that that's just bureaucracy gone mad, remember how many pieces of work are being handed in each week and how much marking that represents. Try managing that with an 'anything goes' philosophy and you'd soon be gridlocked.

---

2 This is demonstrated in the DIY task on p. 37.

Organizing your writing over time

TASK: Below is the time 'wedge', which defines the time you will have to spend on your assignment.

Planning and Preparation →→→→→→→

Production→→→→→→→→→→→

Submission →→→→→→

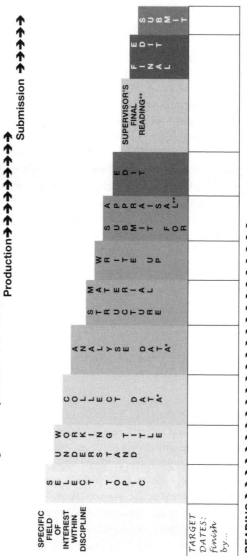

READING→→→→→→→→→→→→→→→→→→→→→→→→→→→→→

DEVELOPING REFERENCE LIST – GLOSSARY – APPENDICES →→→→

Leave time for changes and printing/binding as appropriate

* Data = every kind of information   ** For thesis according to institutional practice

It's better to think of deadlines as working in your favour. If you know that a piece of work has to be in on date X, that gives you a fixed mark from which to work backwards and map out a schedule.

We've illustrated a timescale schedule on p. 30 but, once again, you shouldn't take our divisions as THE way to divide up your schedule; they're just an illustration of the process. In basic terms, you know that you have to:

- Understand the title.
- Work out what it means.
- Decide what materials you need and find out where you can get them or alternatives to them – this might be from your library or through ATHENS[3] or the Internet. (Be careful, though – not everything you get from the Internet is reliable. Much of it hasn't been independently checked for content and accuracy.)
- Do the reading and note-making.
- Organize a plan.
- Write a first draft.
- Give yourself a break.
- Edit the first draft.
- Do a final proofread.
- And hand it in.

It's up to you to decide how much time to give to each of these activities. A pattern such as research (30 per cent), planning (15 per cent), writing (30 per cent), editing (20 per cent) and proofreading (5 per cent) seems reasonable, but that'll depend on your particular strengths and preferences. When you've decided what works best for you, simply start with the handing-in date, work back to the present and divide the time available between the various tasks.

DIY

Assignment time management

But surely that's making things worse. Now, instead of just one deadline, you've got ten. Think about it, though. If you had to choose between two mountaineering expeditions, which would you go for, the one whose plan started with details of the provisions and equipment you'd need, and the route to Base Camp 1? Or the one whose plan simply said 'Climb Everest'?

---

3 If you're unfamiliar with ATHENS, you'll find an explanation of what it is and an indication of how it works on p. 43, but your university library staff will be able to give you specific guidance.

Style and conventions

Style is a complex issue, and we've given it two separate chapters, but there are some basics to consider at this early stage. For the most part, academic writing tends to be impersonal. In other words, as we've already said,[4] you should avoid using expressions such as 'I think that . . .', 'In my opinion . . .' or 'It seems to me that . . .'. To begin with, it's obvious that what you're writing is what you think – after all, it's your assignment. The tone you want to achieve is one that suggests you're presenting objective evidence in support of arguments rather than intuitions and opinions.

Having said that, however, it's important to note that some departments don't mind the subjective approach. They welcome (or tolerate) a more discursive, or more open style. And that's the point of this section. We can't give you any distinct rules because they'll vary from one department to another. So, find out what's acceptable and what isn't. Here are some starter questions to get you thinking:

- Are you allowed to say 'I' in your essay?
- Do you have to use the third person ('one' or 'the researcher') instead?
- Should you prefer the passive to the active voice? (In other words, should you write 'It was decided that . . .' rather than 'We decided that . . .'?)
- Can you use sub-headings?
- Can you use bullet points?
- Are you allowed/encouraged to give your opinion in your conclusion?
- Is there a prescribed way of formatting an essay?
- Should you use explanatory notes?
- If so, should they be footnotes (at the bottom of the page) or endnotes (at the end of the document)?
- Is there a preferred format for citing the books that relate to your work?
- Should you list them as a bibliography or simply a reference list? (And do you know the difference?)
- Does the department have a referencing style sheet that tells you what's approved and what isn't?

---

4 See DIY task on pp. 22–3.

And, while we're on the subject of referencing style sheets, find out which of the main academic ones your department or university prefers. There are several to choose from and the one that's prescribed may depend on which academic discipline you're studying. Four of the most popular ones are the Chicago (superscript number), Vancouver (numerical), Harvard (author, date), and MLA (name, page) methods or styles and they help with such things as standardizing how you introduce quotations and how to format your sources in your bibliography or reference list.[5]

Here's a quick example of how you might use information from a book and identify your source. In this case, the book is an imaginary one; it's called *The Student Writing Guide*. It was written by W. Kirton and K. McMillan and published in 2006 in Dundee by Tayforth Press. The relevant extract reads:

> Students often find that there is little relationship between what they are learning in the theory of their courses and the practice they will meet when they are employed. However, this theoretical foundation provides them with a base from which to address problems that they may encounter as graduates employed within their professional fields.

You don't want to quote the whole thing so, first, you rewrite it in your own words:

> Kirton and McMillan (2006) assert that while students perceive there to be little correlation between theory and practice, once in employment they will find that their theoretical knowledge does, in fact, underpin the way they work.

So, what's happened? You haven't used Kirton and McMillan's words, but you've used their ideas, and the fact that you've told your reader where they came from indicates both that you've read the literature relevant to your subject and that you've acted professionally in acknowledging your source. Whether you agree with the authors or

---

5 In this book, we've chosen to follow the recommendations of the Harvard style sheet but, as we've said, there are differences between the various methods so it's vital that you find out which one your department prefers. Once you've done that, make sure that you always apply it consistently throughout your work.

think they're writing rubbish, you still can't use their words or ideas without identifying them by name in your text and also including the book in the reference list. Using the Harvard method, the entry in the list would be formatted as:

> Kirton, W. and McMillan, K., 2006. *The student writing guide*. Dundee: Tayforth Press.[6]

Layout and presentation

Throughout this book, we'll be stressing that you should always remember that you're writing to be read. You want to get readers on your side, make it as easy as possible for them to understand what you're writing and make them feel comfortable. Pages with curling edges and coffee stains won't do the trick. Also, it's important for the person marking an exercise to have room in which to write any comments or suggestions. Anything that gets in the way of ease of reading and comprehension will count against you. That's why presentation is an important part of the work you're doing. Don't hand in pages that look crowded, where words are crammed together in dense, endless paragraphs. Open up your text. Nowadays, apart from exams, hand-written assignments are rare but, if that's the way you have to hand one in, make sure it's clean, clearly legible and that you leave spaces between the lines. Most importantly, remember to put your name and/or matriculation number on the top sheet of your work. Whether you put your name or not will depend on whether your university operates an anonymous marking scheme.

If you're printing out an assignment, print on one side of the paper, use one-and-a-half or double-line spacing and show a clear separation between paragraphs. (But, as a little aside, don't be fooled by a print-out of a first draft. Any jumble of words, even the weirdest gobble-degook, can look impressive when it's printed out with justified margins and all the associated formatting. Your first draft may, of course, be brilliant; but make sure, before you hand it in, that it doesn't just look good but that it is good.)

---

6 You'll find a fuller explanation of bibliographies and reference lists in Ch. 3, pp. 47–8 and in the QR section, pp. 130–2.

The tutor again

From all of this, you can see that the word 'assignment' can mean several different things. If you're not sure what's required of you, check any departmental handouts you may have been given or, once again, ask your tutors. You may find that attitudes vary between them, even in the same department. So find out what you can expect from them. Are they prepared to read a sample or an early draft? (Unlikely – they simply don't have the time.) Are they prepared to discuss the topic? Are they more interested in your own original ideas or in how well you handle the critical material you've gathered? Do they have any specific requirements in terms of style, structure or presentation? But remember, the university context is different from that of schools. At school, you could probably expect teachers to have a significant amount of input into what you were writing, suggesting approaches, recommending alterations and contributing ideas for you to investigate. At university, you're expected to take full responsibility for your own work and get into the habit of being independent. Tutors have got lots of other students to look after, so don't waste their time.

So, we're two chapters into a book on writing and we still haven't suggested that you write anything. But that's the point – we're dealing with the whole process as a series of steps, each of which makes the following ones easier. So far, we've decided what we need to write about, how we need to write it and where to start looking for the relevant material. But it's still not time to write because, before you do that, you have to do some reading. And that, too, is a skill that can be refined.

DIY TASK I

Using sub-headings

Even if your department discourages the use of sub-headings, you can still use them during the drafting stages of your assignment to help keep yourself orientated. Let's imagine you're writing an essay about medical ethics and that one of its sections examines attitudes to euthanasia. To help you organize the different parts of your argument, you might have sub-headings such as:

- The situation in other European countries.

- The stated policy of the British Medical Association.

- The legal implications.

- The attitudes of individual doctors.

- The testimony of patients.

- The role of carers and relatives.

- The ultimate responsibility.

If you want to check or change the nature and flow of your argument, it's much easier to do so by looking at a list of headings and moving them around rather than having to read through lots of text. But, when you've done that, it's just as easy to absorb the headings into the text by rewriting them as introductory, linking or terminal sentences. For example, the first two headings in this case might become:

- The differing attitudes expressed in other European countries confirm that there is no universal answer to the problem.

And:

- In the UK, the position of health professionals is outlined in the stated policy of the British Medical Association.

Now try doing this with the other headings. Remember, they may serve as transitions between threads as well as being introductions to a new one.

DIY TASK 2

The naked sentence

What follows is a single (badly composed) sentence. To help heighten your awareness of the effectiveness of cutting, try to reduce it to:

- first, the smallest possible sentence without losing the meaning;
- second, the smallest possible coherent sentence.

You can cut UP TO three words at a time, and you're not allowed to add anything or change any of the punctuation. Each time, the words that remain must form a grammatically correct sentence that makes sense.

First, here's an example of reducing the length of a sentence and retaining the meaning:

- Animals that are kept in zoos are often too large for the enclosures in which they are kept and, thus, fail to thrive as they might have done in the wild.
- Animals in zoos are often too large for the enclosures in which they are kept and, thus, fail to thrive as they might have done in the wild.
- Animals in zoos are often too large for the enclosures in which they are kept and, thus, fail to thrive as they might have done.
- Animals in zoos are often too large for the enclosures in which they are kept and, thus, fail to thrive as they might.
- Animals in zoos are often too large for enclosures in which they are kept and fail to thrive as they might.
- Animals in zoos are often too large for enclosures in which they are kept and fail to thrive.

This second example reduces the length but the meaning changes:

- The cars in this street are parked haphazardly and are causing obstructions.
- The cars in this street are parked and are causing obstructions.
- The cars are parked and are causing obstructions.
- The cars are parked and are obstructions.
- The cars are parked.

Now you try.

- According to critics, the works in question tend to rely heavily on explicit contrasts in order to achieve their various effects, setting out, as they do, elaborate, multi-faceted systems which use fundamental physical processes (such as magnetic attraction and repulsion) to produce starkly defined delineations of sound, movement and the purely visual static elements from which the project's overall complexity and impact, ultimately, is created.

DIY TASK 3

Assignment time management

Make a copy of the time 'wedge'. Then, by hand, plot in dates and weeks to outline how you'll need to organize your work within the time frame. You will find the original 'wedge' on p. 30.

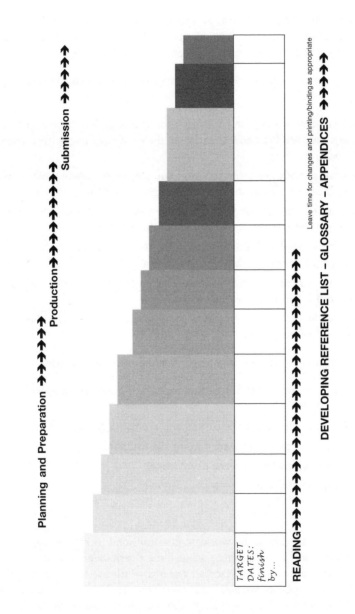

Chapter 3

Read right,
write right

Reading is writing

Now that we know what we need and how we're going to organize it to suit departmental and university requirements, it seems that all we have to do is collect the relevant information. In a way that's true, but one of the many positive aspects of writing at university is that it encourages, even requires you to go further than that.

Information comes ready-packaged nowadays. Never have so many people had such wide and easy access to it. But accessing it is one thing, using it is another. Writing is more than just cutting and pasting. It's not enough to collect quotations, statistics, ideas and the rest, and stick them together; you've got to be able to use the material, adapt it, link it with other pieces of information from other sources. And, to do that, you need to move beyond the surface of the words and think about the underlying ideas and meaning. In other words, think critically.[1] That means comparing ideas and quotations and making a choice between them, preferring the one which is more apt. It means thinking not just about the point you're making but about the other side of the argument, alternative interpretations of a principle or theory. Don't just accept something as true because you found it in a book; challenge the idea, test its validity. Don't just identify what's important in the context of the task you've been set, ask yourself why and how it's important. Get inside the texts you read.

It's like the process of editing film or video; a scene is shot from various angles, favouring different perspectives, emphasizing different

---

1 This 'critical thinking' process began when you were breaking down the assignment title earlier. (See p. 9.)

aspects of what's happening but, in the edit suite, the material is reviewed, selections are made and then spliced together to create a fluid 'real' representation of events. The editor creates a 'reality' on the screen that never actually happened as a single episode. You want to create the same sense of flow, blend selected pieces of the information you've collected into a single, coherent sequence, create your own, unique written 'reality'.

That's what you're doing when you're preparing your assignment. You collect your raw material and you manipulate it to suit your needs. It's not enough to acquire it, you've got to be prepared to select from it and discard what doesn't support or further your argument. So reading is much more than the acquisition of ideas, it also involves comprehension, analysis, organization. It's an integral part of the process of writing. As you read books, articles, websites, your understanding of them is directly influenced by the words their writers use, the way they choose to present their conclusions. In order to understand and accept or reject their arguments, you need to develop a sensitivity to the way they're articulated, an appreciation of how they achieve their effects. And, even though you may not be aware of it, this will influence your own style and approach. You'll see how well-structured writing is easier to understand and, usually, more persuasive, and you'll be able to use some of the techniques you identify to improve your own writing. If you like, thinking critically about what you read is part of your writing apprenticeship. That's what we mean when we say 'reading is writing'.

QR

Structuring arguments and counter-arguments

One familiar problem is that the writers of articles and books can often seem to find much clearer, 'better' ways of expressing your ideas than you do. You have a vague notion about a particular aspect of the issue you're considering and, suddenly, you read a passage that pins it down precisely and accurately. When that happens, instead of feeling frustrated at the 'loss' of something you thought was original, congratulate yourself on having your perception confirmed by an expert, and analyze the wording to see why and how it works so well. The reaction to coming across a sentence that makes you say 'I knew that' should be one of pleasure. It's good to see your own ideas properly expressed and it'll help you to refine them.

Reading, of almost any sort, is good for you and, although we're about to suggest ways of reducing the amount of time you devote to it when you're working to a tight schedule, we believe that it's fundamental not only to education but to experience as a whole. Reading increases your vocabulary, stimulates your thinking and leads you to other places and into the minds of other people. And it makes you a better writer.

Strategic reading

Having said all that, however, we're now going to help you to read less. The reality of the task facing you is that you have a piece of work to hand in and a limited amount of time to complete it. So, as we said in Chapter 2, you need to work to a plan. Sitting in a library reading thousands of words may be good for you, but it takes time. Some people even extend it as much as possible, convincing themselves that they need to do more research whereas, in fact, they're using it as an excuse to put off the actual business of writing. By all means read for pleasure, for enlightenment, for specific research purposes but if your reading relates to the need to write an exercise make it fit the time you've allocated to it. It may be that, when you come to organize or write up your ideas, you find that you need to check some facts or fill some gaps, so you'll need to read some more. But, again, that will be targeted reading.

So, manage your time, keep your focus, concentrate on getting the material that's relevant to your work.

Where should you look?

It's unlikely that you'll be given a topic about which you know nothing and, even if that seems to be the case, there'll always be some indication of where to start looking for enlightenment. There'll be a class reading list and, probably, recommendations made in a lecture or by other students. But you may have to start work on an assignment before you get any lectures, seminars, lab sessions or practicals on that topic, so you need to be ready to look for the relevant books and articles yourself.

When you start searching for them, you'll find that they, in turn, have reference sections leading you to other books and journals on the same topic or theme. And, once you've searched the online library catalogue, you can locate the relevant section in the university library and browse through online periodicals (journals) and e-books for more of the same. You'll find that there's usually far more than you'll need, so make a list of the sources that are most important and likely to be most useful for the exercise in hand.

Deciding what you need to read will depend on what you know already about a topic. If your knowledge is a bit thin, it might be useful first of all to look at more general sources. A good, full-sized dictionary is an obvious starting place. It'll help you to define the terms of the title and refine the aspects of it you need to investigate. Another equally obvious starting place is your own lecture and tutorial notes, or a good general textbook which gives the wider outlines of a subject without going into too much detail. The same is true of a good encyclopaedia, such as the *Encyclopaedia Britannica* (*Micropedia* and *Macropedia*), where you'll find articles on almost everything.

Online, of course, there's *Wikipedia* (www.wikipedia.org), but use it with care. It's interesting, eclectic and, because its entries can be updated more easily and more frequently than those of print encyclo-paedias, may contain more useful or more relevant information. But it's possible that some entries could be regarded as too subjective to be trusted. They may also have been written by people with no specialist knowledge of the subject. Always cross-check.

If your needs are more specific, it might be worth looking in your library reference section for an encyclopaedia of science and technology or language or law – whatever your specialist area is – because often there are specialist encyclopaedias or dictionary reference books that give immediately accessible, clear definitions. Many ordinary textbooks don't include such definitions, but there are others that do have specialist glossaries. For scientific and medical topics, or those concerned with engineering, a specialist dictionary, such as the *Chambers Dictionary of Science and Technology*, will help you to check that your understanding of the meanings of subject-specific words is appropriate in the context of the exercise.

Then there's the Internet. But there's one important point to make about the information you get there. It's crammed with data on every topic imaginable, all of which is relatively easy to find through search engines. But, unlike books, articles and reading lists, which steer you in specific, useful directions, it doesn't have a tight focus. It tends to rely on pop-ups and associations that aren't always relevant. For this and other reasons, you should use it with care. Not all of it is reliable. There are special-interest groups which post versions of historical, social, scientific and political 'facts' that are very one-sided and don't bear much scrutiny. And, even when the information presented is offered in good faith and with an attempt at objectivity, much of it hasn't been independently checked for content and accuracy. So by all means use it, but do so with discretion, and make sure you verify your findings before presenting them as part of your argument.

Online dictionaries also can be helpful, but be careful. They often use non-British English in their spelling and interpretation of words. Your library may have a subscription for a respected British English dictionary such as the *Shorter Oxford English Dictionary* which provides comprehensive coverage of meaning, pronunciation and usage.

> **QR**
>
> Alternative sources of information

The next phase (or the first, if you've already got a basic grasp of the topic), is to look at more specialized textbooks and articles. There you'll find more detailed discussions, more precise information, more complex explanations, and the latest thinking, which may offer new evidence on the question or even challenge the accepted wisdom.

One resource that's particularly useful is ATHENS. It gives you access to many other resources that are available electronically. These can include e-books and e-journals, which have all been refereed by experts and therefore have greater validity than some material available on the wider Internet. ATHENS is available through university libraries. The universities subscribe to it and you can get access by applying to your university library for a unique password. It's valid for your current year of study and it lets you consult a vast array of journals. Whether you're allowed to download or view full-text versions will depend on which journals your library subscribes to; sometimes all you can see is the abstract (that's a summary of the full text). Potentially, it's an excellent resource but it has a downside. Journal articles, for example, are written by subject experts and they're often highly specialized and restricted in the area of the topic they cover. If you rely exclusively on these resources, you might miss out on getting a broader understanding of a topic and, in a wider, end-of-module assessment, this 'gap' in your understanding might let you down. So, use e-resources available through ATHENS selectively and with discretion. Don't rely exclusively on them, back up your findings by referring to your basic text books.

Read efficiently

Even such a brief outline of possible sources suggests that there's a lot of reading to be done. It makes sense, therefore, to read efficiently. If you can train yourself to do that, you can both save time and become more familiar with the relevant issues because you'll be reading only what's essential for you to understand the topic.

So what do we mean by 'efficient' readers? Well, the ones who've decided exactly what they do and don't need to read for the purposes of the assignment and how they're going to read it.

Strategic reading for an assignment starts by establishing what you know already and where you want to go. Look at your list of sources and make a conscious decision about why you should read a particular book, chapter or article and what you expect you'll get out of it. Then, deliberately choose what you're going to read and what you'll leave aside on this occasion. For example, if your background knowledge is thin, it would be a waste of time, and very frustrating, to force yourself to wade through a text that's not making much sense to you.

When you've decided what you're going to read, be selective in the way you work through it. Remember that you're following a schedule, so, however interesting or gripping a particular book may be, make yourself read only the sections of it that are relevant to the present exercise. We're not suggesting that you should only ever read bits of books – just that, in this specific instance, you're reading for a single, defined purpose, so stick to it (and come back and read the rest when you've got more time). Read relevant chapters; look at indexes to find specific references to material that you need; keep your focus tight.

QR

Using an
index

How to read

So, you've decided WHAT you're going to read – now, HOW do you read it? Before you begin, think about what you know already and what you want to find out from the particular text. Next, skim over the whole thing, just to get the general outline of what it's saying. Skimming means moving your eyes quickly over the text, looking for key words and ideas and getting a feel for the main points. You don't yet need to bother with the finer details.

Now look at the first sentence of each paragraph. It's sometimes called the topic sentence and, usually, it helps you to identify what the whole paragraph's about. Don't try making any notes until you've looked at a whole sequence of topic sentences. Then, if you need to, turn the text over or put it to one side and try to jot down its key points to create your own version of how the text's structured. This is part of the critical thinking process we mentioned earlier.[2] Again, don't worry

2 See p. 39.

about details yet, you can fill them in later and use them to expand this first sketch. A natural tendency is to start writing notes as soon as you open a book, but try to avoid doing that. You'll end up making more and more notes as you get tired and find it less and less easy to decide what is and isn't relevant. Apart from wasting time, such a semi-automatic process means that you won't really be thinking about what you're reading, and you won't be learning much from it.

Now that you've got a rough idea of the content and shape of the material, you may decide that you don't need to read it again because it isn't relevant to your research. But if it is relevant, you can go back to it, read it more thoroughly, and make more detailed notes. You'll find that this will be a faster and more meaningful read because you've got a better idea of what you need to look for and where to find it.

By the way, remember what we said in Chapter 1 about trying to develop a system of note-making that uses one piece of card or paper for each item. It'll make it easier to organize material later. Try, too, to be systematic in the way you take notes. Make a careful record of each source you use and remember to include the page number. And it'll make life much easier for you later if you get into the habit of always recording sources in the way that's outlined in the particular style sheet preferred by your department. That'll include such things as the order in which you put the author, title, date, publisher and place of publication, and whether to italicize or underline the title. In the case of periodicals, you must also note the volume number and page numbers. If you don't, you'll spend valuable time later wondering where something came from, and searching through books and articles in the library.

If you're taking something down as a quotation, make sure you copy it EXACTLY as you find it in the original, even if there are misspellings or other mistakes in it. A suggestion that's sometimes made is that you could maybe use different coloured pens for different types of notes: one for direct quotations, one for general ideas taken from an article or book, one for your own ideas, and so on. That makes it easier for you to identify notes in the future. It also helps you to avoid plagiarism. We'll deal with that important consideration in Chapter 5.

Quoting and citing

It's useful to know the difference between quotations and citations. A quotation consists of words that are copied directly from the original text. A citation refers to information you've taken from another source

QR

Quotations
and
citations

but which you've paraphrased in your own words. In both cases, you must note the author and all the other details of the source at the end of the sentence, unless, of course, you've already used the author's name as part of the structure of the sentence. If, for example, you were using the Harvard method, you'd write 'Jessop (1999) asserts that . . .' It's very important that you include all this information in your bibliography or reference list. If you don't, you may lose marks.

Quotations and citations should all be integrated smoothly into your text. Too many students just rely on dropping them into their work without introduction or explanation and relying on them to make their point. The result can be a barely connected sequence of discrete statements that fail to cohere into a persuasive argument. Quotations and citations are a vital part of academic writing but, wherever possible, you should outline what the idea is in your own words

DIY

Reporting
words

before you introduce them and say why you're using that particular quotation. It may be the perfect expression of what you want to say, but you should still use it as a support for your own point. As long as you identify its source, you won't be guilty of plagiarism, but if your work simply consists of joined up chunks of other people's words, it'll be uneven, it won't really be yours, and the marks are likely to reflect that fact.

Modality

Modals are auxiliary verbs, which means they're used with other verbs. They convey possibility, probability, certainty, permission, requests, instructions, suggestions, offers and invitations, wants and wishes, obligations and necessity.[3] They're frequently used in speech but there's also a place for some of them in academic writing, especially when you need to qualify a point you're making. Notice the difference, for example, between 'The results were compromised by the small turnout' and 'The results may have been compromised by the small turnout'. Using the modal protects you. It allows you to distinguish between certainty, probability and possibility.

Modals also help you to avoid making value judgements.[4] The claim

---

3 Some examples are 'We could test the results', 'It might be possible to organize', 'They were able to confirm the findings'.
4 We deal with value judgements in more detail in Ch. 7, pp. 100–1 and the DIY task on p. 110.

that 'Nurses are dedicated to providing the best possible level of care for their patients' is a statement of opinion, not fact. You can't prove that every single nurse has that degree of commitment. It is, however, legitimate to write 'Nurses may be dedicated to providing the best possible level of care for their patients' or 'Nurses should be dedicated to providing the best possible level of care for their patients'. In some contexts, modals may give the impression that they're 'weakening' the main verb – 'it is' is much 'stronger' than 'it may be' – but when your statements must be supported by evidence, not conjecture, it's safer to convey them through the nuances of modals.

DIY

Modality

Bibliographies and reference lists

Having consulted these disparate books and articles, it's essential that you include them all in a bibliography or a reference list. A bibliography lists all the books, journals and other source material you've consulted to help you to prepare your paper and, in some disciplines, it's what your marker will expect to see. A reference list, which is sometimes called a list of citations, identifies all the source material that you've actually quoted or cited in your paper. You may have consulted other sources that have affected your understanding of the subject, but if they're not actually cited in your work, some departments don't expect you to include them.

QR

Bibliographies and reference lists

A lot of time can be wasted trying to remember where you found a quotation or an idea so, when you're making notes, always add the source and page number to them and make sure you take down all the details you'll need for your bibliography or reference list. You might find it useful to set up a sort of template document that starts with an example of the recommended formatting. Then, as you read books and articles, you can add them to the list, making sure they're set out in exactly the same way. There are software packages that provide templates to help you with referencing.

It may seem a time-consuming exercise, but it's important to take it seriously. Academic writing has some clear rules and they have to be followed. A reference list acknowledges the fact that you've used other people's work. Even if you've quoted or cited something simply to disagree with it, you've still used someone else's intellectual property and you must show that you recognize this. You're part of a community that thrives on sharing knowledge and prides itself on respecting and valuing the ideas of other people.

Bibliographies and reference lists also help your readers and markers to understand how you put your argument together and what influenced your thinking. They can see how much you've read, what material you've chosen, and judge for themselves the relevance of your reading and the skill you've used to identify sources that have contributed to your presentation. This may help them to assess your work and suggest further reading or sources that are more relevant. It'll also help them to form their own opinions of what you've written.

Remember the basics

We've been mentioning efficiency in terms of collecting relevant material and managing your time. There's another area where efficiency is important: your eyesight. If you're having difficulties reading or if you think you're a slow reader, it wouldn't hurt to get your eyes tested.

And, if your eyes are fine, but you're just a slow reader, don't let it bother you. Everyone's different. Some people may seem to read faster, but they may not understand or remember what they've read as well as you do. It's not a speed reading competition; it's an exercise in comprehension and, one hopes, enlightenment. And, if a text is difficult, you'll need to take more time with it and read it more slowly anyway, to make sure that you understand it. If you don't, you're wasting your time. Of course, if you're having difficulty with a text, it may be because it's not very well written. If that's the case, it might be worth looking for something that's more reader-friendly. You can always go back to the more difficult text once you've got a better grasp of the principles or concepts.

Try to get into the habit of doing the sort of 'text survey' we mentioned – the quick skim, topic sentence approach. And, when you start the detailed read, don't let your eyes start wandering away from the line you're currently reading, looking for something else. And don't start reading with your pencil poised all ready to make notes. Read first, think about it, recall it and then write your notes.

Finally, if you come across any unfamiliar words the first time you're reading through a passage, don't stop and look them up right away. Keep on skimming the text to get its gist. If you need to, jot the words down on a piece of paper and look them up after you've finished your general survey. It might also be useful to keep a list of them in case they crop up in the future.

In this chapter, we've necessarily had to turn reading into a self-limiting, structured exercise. The danger of such an approach is that it devalues the process of reading itself. Most of the emphasis in this book is on the various aspects of writing, but that doesn't diminish the central importance of reading. As we said, reading is writing. Capturing and absorbing the ideas of others, stretching your own mental horizons, joining the community of minds that are represented in the pages of books and journals – all these activities add to your skills, sharpen your perceptions and give you access to experiences that may be unfamiliar but will help you to develop, not only as a student but as a person.

DIY TASK 1

'Reporting' words

There are different ways of introducing the ideas of others into your text. However, as critical thinkers, it may be that we're drawing attention to the work of others because we want to criticize rather than agree with it. It may be that a particular piece of research evidence isn't yet widely accepted and so it's the subject of debate. This means that the word we choose to introduce the ideas we want to cite becomes important as a sort of subliminal signal about what we think of them. The verbs in the list that follows are frequently used in academic writing such as textbooks and journals. You might like to mark up the ones that sound as if the writer agrees with the source and those she might use to distance herself from the viewpoint she's citing. You may feel that there's a further category where it seems as if there's some doubt about the idea that's being presented, or perhaps that a word could be used in more than one context. The aim is just to encourage you to think about your choice of word so that what you write is actually what you mean. Again, if you don't know some of these words, it would be useful to look them up.

		Agreement	Disagreement	Doubt			Agreement	Disagreement	Doubt
1	... advanced the view that				16	... guessed that			
2	... affirmed that				17	... held the view that			
3	... alleged that				18	... insisted that			
4	... asserted that				19	... judged that			
5	... averred that				20	... opined that			
6	... believed that				21	... posited the view that			
7	... claimed that				22	... proclaimed that			
8	... commented that				23	... professed that			
9	... contended that				24	... proposed that			
10	... declared that				25	... questioned the view that			
11	... decreed that				26	... stated that			
12	... defined				27	... suggested that			
13	... established that				28	... supposed that			
14	... explained that				29	... surmised that			
15	... expounded the view that				30	... warned that			

DIY TASK 2

Modality

The following sentences can be seen as too assertive, even too dogmatic in their directness. Use modality to soften their directness and make them more reasonable and more persuasive:

- It was convenient for Sartre to adapt his existentialist beliefs to accommodate the need for political commitment but that weakened him as both thinker and activist.

- In order to determine the relative strength of two acids, we compare their pKa values but, if the need is to base the comparison on an organic structure alone, consulting a pKa table does not provide sufficient information.

- Convictions in criminal cases depend on the reliability of witnesses. They have their own agendas, their memory of events is flawed and, if they have any connection with the victim, their desire to help the police significantly influences the direction their statements take. They are less concerned with saying what they saw and more intent on condemning the perpetrators of the crime. Psychological evaluations have shown that, when being questioned by a lawyer who is hostile to them, they become more dogmatic and assertive in their replies.

Chapter 4

Creating a plan

Structuring skills

At last we've arrived at the point where you'll begin to compose the assignment. You're still not going to be doing any actual writing, but the next step is the one that will make the whole task easier. And it'll involve several different types of activity, all of which are identified in a well-known set of categories known as *Bloom's Taxonomy*. Benjamin Bloom was an educational psychologist who, in 1956, created his *Taxonomy of Educational Objectives*. The psychologists among you will be comfortable with its terminology as it deals with overlapping cognitive, psychomotor, and affective domains and behavioural paradigms but, as we keep on saying, we value clarity above everything else and so we'll try to make it more generally accessible.

Taxonomy means classification, and educational objectives include any activities that help us to learn so, in very crude terms, we're dealing with a list of six types of mental activity organized into lower and higher learning skills. That's a gross over-simplification but our aim is simply to understand the processes involved, not analyse or evaluate Bloom's work. The six categories are labelled:

- knowledge
- comprehension
- application
- analysis
- synthesis
- evaluation.

This chapter is about using them to create a detailed plan for your piece of work.

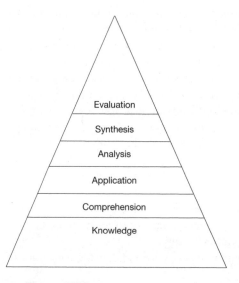

Bloom's taxonomy (Bloom, 1956)

You could think of them as a pyramid, as in the figure above. The base, the lowest order, is knowledge and its meaning is self-evident. It's the processing of information, which involves activities such as observing, identifying and remembering.

The next level, comprehension, introduces the notion of understanding the information. It's still considered to be a lower order skill but it's a step up; with comprehension, you don't just memorize facts, you know what they mean. You've processed the knowledge and deposited it in your awareness bank.

The next progression brings us to the middle two layers of the pyramid. is the ability to take material that you've learned and understood and use it in other appropriate contexts and new situations. Analysis involves using knowledge, comprehension and application to understand structure, patterns and relationships, to organize material and recognize hidden meanings and to look at things from a variety of different angles.

When you can do all this, you're equipped to use information and ideas to create new patterns, new structures. In other words, you can use old ideas to create new ones. That's the process of synthesis, which lets you take a set of facts, choose the ones that are most relevant to the task in hand, and draw general conclusions from them.

Finally, at the top of the pyramid, comes evaluation. This is the highest level of thinking, and it uses all the other five elements to make judgements, compare ideas and draw distinctions between them, assess their value, and make informed choices based on evidence.

So these are the skills that you're now going to use to organize the material you've collected into the structural framework of your essay. By identifying and finding what you needed, you've already moved through the first two stages – information and comprehension – it's time to move on up through the other four by:

- choosing material and putting it in different relationships (application);
- recognizing the new ideas that these relationships create (analysis);
- putting these ideas together to form the unique substance of your essay (synthesis); and
- weighing up the evidence and drawing conclusions from it (evaluation).

This process is, of course, the preparation for the actual writing of the assignment, which may seem to suggest that it's 'only' a preliminary task. But it's important to recognize that, if you do it thoroughly and conscientiously, it'll make the writing much easier. You'll be more familiar with the material, know where it's leading, and spend far less time wondering what to write.

Getting organized

Our starting point is the material you've accumulated so far. Basically, it's a pile of notes, quotations, ideas, references – the unstructured substance of your assignment. It's got no shape, form, argument or coherence. It's just a lot of words about your subject, some contradicting one another, some repeating one another, some maybe not relevant at all. So the first thing to do is start imposing some order on it. The trouble is that it looks just as difficult as it did when we started because there's so much of it. So where do we begin?

Some say that this is the stage at which you should think up a theme, make a plan, jot down headings and sub-headings. If that suits you, fine, do it. But the problem there is that, until you've sifted through all the material, it's not obvious how powerful your arguments might be one way or the other. You also might find that, having decided that your plan is going to prove one thing, the evidence you've gathered could lead you in a totally different direction. So, instead of trying once again to confront a major task, let's do what we said at the beginning and turn the whole exercise into a series of smaller tasks. Let's start making the material do the work for us.

You're all studying different topics, using different disciplines and terminologies. Some of you will be analyzing linguistic variables, others interpreting Minoan artefacts, others measuring the half-life of sub-atomic particles or describing bacterial action in anoxic environments. The variables may not be infinite, but they're far too numerous for us to cover here. Whatever your discipline – engineering, physics, graphic design, medicine, literature, music – you've gathered a heap of material specific to the task facing you, and we obviously can't give you examples relevant to each particular subject. So, we're going to have to use a catch-all image to make it simpler.

The heap of material you have to organize consists of many different aspects of the subject. If you imagine that each of those aspects is a different colour, you have a jumbled, multi-coloured heap. What you need to do is sort it out so that the various colours are no longer mixed up, but separated into more easily discernible heaps. In simplistic terms, then, and for the sake of convenience, let's represent the different aspects of your topic by colours and assume that those colours make up the subject matter of your assignment.

So, we've got a pile of quotations, ideas, references and notes all relating in some way to the 'colours' you've selected. The first step towards structuring the assignment is to take just one of the bits of material from the pile and decide what it's about. So pick out any note, read it and decide which category it belongs in. Let's assume that it relates somehow to the colour red.

We create a file called RED and put the piece of material in it. When we say create a file, it can be on the computer or an actual file, or even just a pile on your desk, the floor, your bed, the fridge or wherever – as long as you've got a distinct space that, as you're organizing material, is reserved for the colour red.

Now take the next piece of material from the pile. If that, too, relates to red, put it with the other one. If not, decide what colour is relevant and create another file, say BLUE. And follow the same technique as you work your way through the pile.

Don't try to evaluate any of the material at this stage. All you're doing is taking it from the shapeless mass into which you first put it and creating a set of smaller, more coherent masses. It's true that each of them is still shapeless but at least we now know that the items in each one do belong together and are about the same thing.

And just keep doing this until the one large pile has become several small ones. It perhaps sounds a little mechanical but, just by reading each item and having to decide where to put it, you'll also be forcing yourself to become more familiar with your material, understand it better and start evaluating its significance.[1]

Building a structure

So, where we had a big pile with no label before, we now have several piles, each with a label – RED, BLUE, GREEN, PINK, etc. It's the same material, of course, but it's been sorted out into more manageable pieces so that we can start building some structure into it.

For most of us, structure isn't a natural aspect of our thinking. Thoughts come and go, sometimes linked with one another, sometimes veering off at tangents. It's only when we consciously decide to create a sequence that we're forced to impose what's essentially an artificial shape on our ideas. And, paradoxically, it's that artificiality that makes them 'real'. For example, if we now ask you to think of 'water', you may imagine anything from a half-empty bath to an ocean, with ponds, icebergs, and bottles of fizzy stuff on supermarket shelves in between. If, however, we choose 'running water', that eliminates associations such as lakes, puddles and ice cubes, but it still allows a range stretching from Niagara to a teapot pouring. 'Hot running water' restricts your options further. 'Clean water' or 'dirty water' introduces the possibility of contrasts and comparisons, and the more closely we define the element, the more we restrict the risk of being misunderstood.

Precision in language is clearly important and, if there's so much potential for confusion with a substance as 'ordinary' as water, consider the possible mental mayhem if we're discussing abstract notions, such as ethics or thought itself. We use language and context to pin down our ideas and clarify them so that there's less danger of them being misinterpreted by others. In other words, we take the shapeless, elusive thoughts in our heads and wrap them in words to make them accessible as distinct, discernible, external realities. That's what you're aiming to

---

1 By the way, it's not always possible (or wise) to include every scrap of information or data that you've gleaned from your reading. Think critically, be selective – sometimes less is more.

do when writing your assignment. You want to articulate your ideas clearly, link them with care, put them into an unambiguous context, and communicate to your reader the exact shape of your argument.

In this case, the thoughts and ideas that make up our argument are actually laid out before us (in the shape of notes), which obviously makes the process a little easier. So, to get back to the task itself, choose just one of the heaps. It doesn't matter which – let's say RED – and start going through it, item by item. For the moment, forget all about BLUE, PINK and the rest. As you start comparing the RED notes with one another, you'll probably find that some of them are repetitive or contradictory. If so, just get rid of the repeats. Don't throw them away. They may be useful for your introduction or conclusion so put them in a file called, for example, RED MISCELLANEOUS or RED EXTRAS or some other label that identifies them clearly. The contradictions, on the other hand, will probably be useful in that they'll help you to make sure your argument is balanced. If all your notes are saying the same thing, that makes for a potentially bland and dull essay.

As you're going through the material, start imposing some order on the items you're keeping. How you do that is up to you. Just read them and see how they fit together, lead into one another, contradict one another, reinforce one another, etc. They're all about RED but, as with 'water', there are many possible associations. Some may refer to things being 'red hot', others to 'an angry red'; there could be references to crimson sunsets, red blood, the red shirts of a football club, a redheaded person, or the red flag of communism. That's good, because it'll help you to break down all your RED notes into what we could call mini-groups within the overall category (RED-HEAT, RED-BLOOD, RED-FOOTBALL, etc.). How they fit together will sometimes be obvious but, equally, there may be some that need a bit more thought before you see how to use them. If that's the case, make a note to remind yourself of how you're linking them and add that at the appropriate place in the pile. It doesn't need to be complicated, just something that triggers the association you made between two notes so that, when you come to write the essay, you don't have to stop to work out the connection all over again.

DIY
Planning the
assignment

Remember, you're still not writing the assignment, you're just organizing your material.

When you've reorganized the pile into its mini-groups, the next step is to put those groups themselves into a coherent sequence, just as you did with the individual notes. Once again, the choice is yours. Decide

DIY

Organizing
an
argument

which group would give the RED section of your assignment
the best start, then choose the one that follows most naturally
on from there, and work through them all, assessing where they
should go, changing them round, trying out different
combinations until you're satisfied that they're in an order that
makes sense. You could use contrasts, conflicts or a gradual,
seamless progression from gentler, muted tones to a strong, fiery
conclusion or vice versa. It just depends on what the essay's asking you
to do and what you want to say.

When you've finished that, you'll have a category (RED) that is no
longer shapeless but has a definite internal structure. You may want to
write this section up at this stage, while all the ideas you've had about
it are still fresh in your mind. If so, that's fine. If you're not sure,
though, leave it. The way you organize the other piles may change the
order you've given this one. Our own preference would be to continue
the process of organizing until the whole structure is in place ready for
the next phase – the writing.

So, to continue with the structuring, forget about RED and start on
one of the other colours, following exactly the same procedure until
you've sorted every mini-group into an ordered, self-contained,
comprehensible sequence. When the last one's complete, you'll have
some discarded, unsorted material (in the MISCELLANEOUS piles),
but also, in place of the shapeless categories that were there before,
you'll have a set of distinct, coherent progressions on which to build
your arguments.

Now, just as you put the individual notes then the mini-groups into
a chosen order, do exactly the same thing with your broader categories.
Once again, it's up to you how you do it. Look at each one, see how
the thread of its meaning develops within it (according to the way
you've organized it), and start putting them together so that the meaning
moves logically, naturally, from one to the other. Again, you may use
contrasts, finishing the RED section on a fiery note and deciding that
the best direction to take is to introduce the coolness of BLUE to
provide a contrast. On the other hand, you may want a more gradual
transition, in which case, you may choose ORANGE. The beauty of
this process is that there's no absolute, foolproof way of doing this; it's
entirely your choice as to what shape you're going to give it. You're
creating something unique. Remember, you're not trying to produce
a 'correct answer', you're manipulating thoughts and language to create
YOUR considered, individual response to a given instruction.

You see how you've let the material do the work for you. **DIY**
You've planned the overall structure for your assignment but,
rather than sit in a vacuum and try to force broad abstractions
into legitimate progressions, you've considered the evidence little
by little and used it to construct the framework on which you'll
write.

Linking
groups

At this stage, it's worth taking a short break before moving
to the actual business of writing. You've put all the categories together,
so go and do something else, start another project, read something
different, or just relax. Then, come back to this task with a clear mind
and check the structure you've created to make sure that it's as strong
as you thought it was. You may want to reconsider and do a bit more
rearranging. Or you may find that there are gaps and that you need to
do a little more reading to fill them. But now you can do that with
more confidence because, as you've been working through these
seemingly minor exercises, you've been getting to know the topic
better and better. At no point have you been consciously dealing with
the overall assignment, but you've been creating it by getting a better
understanding of the material and how it flows. The heap of undiffer-
entiated ideas with which you started has been turned into a sequence
that has coherence and progression. In fact, it's an essay. Now all you
have to do is write it.

DIY TASK 1

Planning the assignment

Look at the QR on spider diagrams, idea clusters and brainstorming on p. 162. The idea cluster is about the value of the Internet as an aid to studying and learning. Think about how you might be able to group some of the ideas in much the same way as you read about in the red, green and blue example in the main text of this chapter.

Below is a list of categories relating to the idea cluster. They may not coincide with your own interpretation of the subject but try using them as headings to classify the points in the diagram:

1 practical aspects

2 generic advantages

3 generic disadvantages

4 learning and studying aspects.

You might find it useful to highlight the items on the idea cluster, pink, yellow, purple, orange, for example, so that you'll have a visual image of the relative strength of argument/information under each of these categories. Once you've done this you could then consider how you might sequence these categories for the writing stage if you had to write this up as an assignment.

DIY TASK 2

Organizing an argument

Each of the points listed below from A to Q represents an element of a brief essay on immigration. If you had to write the essay, the way you sequenced them would depend on the way in which the task requirements were formulated and on how you interpret what's required. Read through the list and then decide on how you'd reorganize the sequence to respond to the essay questions that follow it. It'll help you to see how structure differs according to purpose:

A At one point, the President's office proposed that there might be an amnesty for illegal immigrants.

B Despite its ethnic diversity, the self-image of the USA seems to project the notion of a singular, predominantly 'American' culture.

C EU countries are, willingly or otherwise, welcoming workers from Eastern Europe.

D European criticism of the USA's immigration policies is fundamentally hypocritical.

E Fear of job losses was as important a factor as the loss of national identity for many citizens of Western Europe.

F For some Americans, the influx of different ethnicities appears to run counter to God's intentions.

G Illegal immigration is a crime.

H It could be argued that America is a nation made up entirely of immigrants.

I Multiculturalism is a feature of most societies in the modern world.

J Protests and rallies have been organized to show the strength of feeling of Latinos in various states of the USA.

K The growth of terrorism has caused immigration controls to be tightened everywhere.

L The new South American politics is making the USA more nervous.

M The USA prides itself on being able to absorb and embrace the most varied arrivals.

N The votes of Latinos living in the USA could influence the outcome in some local elections.

O There is a very large Latino population living legally in the USA as well as a significant number of illegal immigrants.

P There is little agreement in Washington about how to control immigration.

Q While patriotism persists, peace will remain elusive.

Possible instructions:

1 Assess the impact of mass immigration on attitudes towards multiculturalism in the USA and Europe.

2 Examine the implications of illegal immigration in the USA and Europe.

3 Increasingly, immigration is becoming a major policy issue in the USA and Europe. Discuss.

4 Consider the view that immigrant communities represent a threat to host cultures.

DIY TASK 3

Linking groups

On p. 36 we gave you a DIY task that consisted of a set of possible sub-headings relating to euthanasia as part of an essay on medical ethics. Your job then was to rewrite them as transitional sentences. We've used the same sequence for this task but, this time, instead of listing the sub-headings, we've written the sentences with which each group of ideas might begin and end and rearranged the groups into a random sequence. Using these sentences as your guide, rearrange the groups into a sequence of paragraphs that flow smoothly into one another to form a coherent, developing sequence. There's no need to write out each paragraph – the object is to practise creating smooth links between them. If necessary, alter the wording to make the transitions easier. Once again, there is no single 'correct' answer. The sentences have been written to allow several possibilities.

Here's an example to help you see what's needed. We'll use group C as our starting point (but we could just as easily have started with any of the others).

It is difficult to identify any social layer that is not touched in some way by the need to confront the issue of euthanasia. (*Development of argument*) Taking refuge in either the strictures of religion or the moral imperatives of the present laws is an abnegation of responsibility; there is a need for serious, informed debate.

In such a debate, many different viewpoints will be represented. In the UK, the position of health professionals is outlined in the stated policy of the British Medical Association. (*Development of argument*) Thus, although the legal position is stated in unequivocal terms, there appears to be room for flexibility in its interpretation.

No discussion of the topic can proceed without first establishing the attitudes of individual doctors. (*Development of argument*) With regard, then, to attitudes towards euthanasia, these findings suggest that the profession is as divided as the population as a whole.

Etc., etc.

Now, you try it.

Group	Opening sentence	Closing sentence
A The legal implications.	If decisions could simply be made according to the conscience of individual medical practitioners, the situation would already be confusing but there is the added complication of their legal implications.	The onus is on the government to conduct a thorough survey of attitudes and, through a process of consultation with the medical and other caring professions, draft a law that recognizes and accommodates these diverse opinions.
B The stated policy of the British Medical Association.	In the UK, the position of health professionals is outlined in the stated policy of the British Medical Association.	Thus, although the legal position is stated in unequivocal terms, there appears to be room for flexibility in its interpretation.
C The ultimate responsibility.	It is difficult to identify any social layer that is not touched in some way by the need to confront the issue of euthanasia.	Taking refuge in either the strictures of religion or the moral imperatives of the present laws is an abnegation of responsibility; there is a need for serious, informed debate.
D The attitudes of individual doctors.	No discussion of the topic can proceed without first establishing the attitudes of individual doctors.	With regard, then, to attitudes towards euthanasia, these findings suggest that the profession is as divided as the population as a whole.
E The situation in other European countries.	The differing attitudes expressed in other European countries confirm that there is no universal answer to the problem.	As a result, when drafting any policy proposals, administrators must always assume that, among the most significant factors to be considered are those of religion and politics.
F The role of carers and relatives.	The resultant hardships extend beyond the sufferers themselves to the carers and relatives charged with looking after them.	It may well be that the resultant tensions exacerbate the situation and make rational assessments impossible.
G The testimony of patients.	When the opinions of patients are sought, they offer no more unanimity than any other section of the population.	It is therefore essential to distinguish between anecdotal and factual evidence before drawing any conclusions about what is perceived to be the greater good.

Joined-up writing

Writing is thinking

This is a book about writing and yet we've only just – in Chapter 5 –
got round to the actual business of beginning to put words together.
That may seem rather late in the day but, as we hope you agree by
now, writing is much more than tapping on keys or tracing letters with
a pen. In a way, you've been doing it from the time you started unpicking
the title of the assignment. Thinking about your material, organizing
it, preparing it – that's all part of the writing process. Writing is thinking,
putting words to thoughts clarifies them, gives them accessible shape.

The point was made very simply by the environmentalist, James
Lovelock, in *The Observer* magazine (Siegle, 22 May 2005: 8). He told
his interviewer, 'In science, if you can't explain what you're doing to
a non-scientist of reasonable intelligence, then you probably don't really
know yourself.' The difference here, of course, is that you're not
communicating with a 'non-scientist' or, indeed, a 'non-anything'. It
may seem bizarre but you're writing about a specialist subject and you're
writing for someone who usually knows more about it than you do.
However, that doesn't change anything. Markers aren't just looking for
facts; they're interested in how you're handling information and how
you're conveying your understanding of it. So don't make assumptions
about how much your reader knows; be clear, lead her through your
argument, and make sure you keep her orientated. Always remember
that you're writing to be read. As you start giving your ideas their
definitive shape and turning the separate notes into a clear, sustained
argument, keep your reader in mind. In very crude terms, you want to
tell her 'this is where we are' and, as you move through the essay,
'that's where we've been and this is where we're heading now'.

Just as there's no single 'right' way of writing an assignment, so there are many ways of presenting an argument. Elsewhere, we've mentioned the differences between the sciences and the humanities[1] but there may be others, even within the same institution. Some conventions may prefer that you fill in the background to a point before you make it while others may want to hear the point first and then be told how you arrived at it. So it's important for you to find out exactly what's needed.

The first draft

We'll deal with general stylistic considerations in the next chapter but, at this point, remember what we wrote in Chapter 2 about subjectivity and the need for an impersonal approach. Don't use expressions such as 'I think that . . .', 'In my opinion . . .', 'It seems to me that . . .'. In fact, don't use 'I' at all unless you're sure that it's acceptable in your discipline.

Writing the first draft is simply a question of working your way systematically through the notes that you've organized with such care. You know that they follow a planned sequence and connect with one another, so simply start with the first note and start moving through the pile, joining them together. If you think of your notes and quotations as the building blocks of your argument, what you're now supplying is the mortar. But, as an image, that leaves a lot to be desired because each trowelful of real mortar is much like every other one whereas the ways in which you link your points are going to be very varied. (Consider, for example, how different that last sentence would have been if we'd written 'and' instead of 'whereas'.) Equally, bricks and mortar are separate substances and there's a clear line between them, while words and sentences that link ideas grow out of and into those ideas and are part of the same texture. It's not enough to write 'and then', 'and then', 'next', 'after that', and so on; you'll need to expand the notes, make sure they have internal coherence and that they flow smoothly, and choose the appropriate words and expressions to join them to one another.

Even at the simplest level, the importance of this choice is clear. Take, for example, two short notes:

- The Treaty negotiations were conducted during the summer.

---

1 See Ch. 2, pp. 26–8.

and:

- The French insisted on including provisions for immediate repatriation.

The meaning of each of these sentences is clear. But the words we use to connect them, however simple, can change the emphasis of their meaning, and even change the meaning itself. The same is true if we change the order of the two notes. The following table shows what we mean:

The Treaty negotiations were conducted during the summer	because in case although and before	the French insisted on including provisions for immediate repatriation.
The French insisted on including provisions for immediate repatriation	therefore and, as a result, which meant that but because	the Treaty negotiations were conducted during the summer.

However powerful your ideas and quotations, they can be weakened and even negated by the words and expressions you use to hold them together. These words and expressions create the path that leads the reader through your thinking, and different paths lead in different directions. The words can be classified as 'signposts'. It's obviously important not to lose your readers. You don't want to take them on a mystery tour; you want them to recognize that they're following a well-prepared, purposeful path. The use of signpost words, such as 'first', 'second', 'in addition', 'conversely', will help them to follow the logic of your thought and the line of argument or discussion. Consider the story of Shakespeare's Othello, whose jealousy led him to kill his innocent wife, Desdemona, and notice the effect of using different signpost words and expressions in the following sentences:

- Othello killed Desdemona BECAUSE he loved her.
- Othello killed Desdemona EVEN THOUGH he loved her.

- Othello killed Desdemona, THUS BELYING HIS CLAIM THAT he loved her.
- Othello killed Desdemona INSISTING THAT he loved her.
- Othello killed Desdemona TO PROVE THAT he loved her.

Each one gives a different emphasis to the murder, implies different motives and justifications and, consequently, alters the nature of the tragedy.

You can see, then, that your choice of linking expression is as important to the flow of your argument as the ideas themselves. If, for example, you wanted to add one idea or statement to another, you might use words and phrases such as 'and', 'moreover', or 'of equal/lesser importance'. The one you choose would define the way in which the two ideas relate to one another. Similarly, if you wanted to compare ideas, you'd get different effects by using 'however', 'nevertheless', 'alternatively', 'but' or 'conversely'. When creating a sequence (say A and B), 'consequently' and 'subsequently' are seen by some as interchangeable; in fact, they have very different implications. 'Consequently' means that B happened as a result of A, 'subsequently' simply means that B happened after A, without there necessarily being any close connection between the two. So be careful how you choose the words you use to bring your ideas together.

QR
'Signpost' words

Constructing paragraphs

Examples of good academic writing tend to follow a recognizable pattern when it comes to paragraph structure. They don't operate to hard and fast rules but they do provide guidelines that you might find it useful to follow. Each paragraph begins with what's known as a topic sentence – that's a sentence which introduces what the paragraph's going to be about. The sentences that follow then develop the ideas leading from that sentence, either expanding it or offering a contrasting view. They lead to the final sentence of the paragraph, which expresses either termination, to sum up the topic, or transition, to link with the next paragraph.

Incidentally, as you're writing, it may be worth noting down on a separate piece of paper the mini-conclusion for each paragraph or group of paragraphs. That'll give you a list of your key points, which you could use when you come to write your overall conclusion. It'll help you to keep your conclusion focused on what you've actually said in the body of the work.

DIY
Structuring paragraphs

You can use the same technique to assess the structure of your own or any other piece of work. By reducing each paragraph to a single bullet point, or even a single word, you can quickly skim through the points to check how an argument develops and see whether there are any gaps. The very process of reducing the paragraph to a single idea makes you more familiar with it, and it's much easier to grasp the broad sweep of a discussion by comparing single line notes than by reading through entire sequences of paragraphs.

Write first, edit later

We're now going to make another artificial distinction and suggest that you treat the actual writing process as two separate tasks – writing and editing. It's artificial because, of course, as you're choosing the words in the first place you're subconsciously editing them to decide what best suits your purpose, but we want to encourage you to write your first draft as freely as possible, without being too critical of yourself. Later, when you switch into edit mode, you can be as severe as you like (in fact, we'll insist that you are). We'll deal with that in Chapter 7.

Of course, writing for a geology department, for example, may be very different from writing for a maths or linguistics department; each has its distinct terminology and, perhaps, a preferred manner of presenting material. But the more you allow yourself to write freely, the more confident you'll become and, once you're in the habit of writing in this way, you'll be better placed to adapt your technique to reproduce the preferred style of your chosen discipline.

So now you're working your way through your notes, linking them into sequences, creating connections and contrasts, adding things to strengthen your arguments, using quotations and citations to reinforce your points, perhaps outlining opposing views then synthesizing their conclusions. And the important thing at this, the writing stage, is to keep the argument and progressions flowing. Don't concern yourself too much with grammar, style or spelling. Not yet. If you start worrying about whether you've chosen the right word or used the right tense, you risk losing the thread of your argument and having to go back through what you've written to pick it up again, all of which wastes time and can lead to weak points appearing, false starts, and/or gaps in the presentation. Of course correct grammar and spelling are import-ant, but we'll deal with that later. For now, you want to make sure that you pin down the structured argument that you worked so hard to organize earlier.

A word of caution, though. We seem to be suggesting that you gallop on, just writing any old thing; that's not the case. If you adopt a conversational tone, or lapse into slang or texting mode, you'll be creating thoughts that won't have the tightness and coherence you need for an academic presentation. Everyday conversations and text messages are mostly loose, approximate processes in which precision isn't usually necessary. They're fine for the purpose of informal contact but not when you're making specific points, supporting them with clearly expressed opinions from other academics and building towards a considered conclusion. If you write an essay in 'text-speak', you'll have to translate it later, which, effectively, means writing it twice. So, don't worry too much about things that interrupt the flow, but be careful to establish approximately the right register (that is, style) from the start. Remember your reader.

Jargon

Jargon sometimes seems very enticing. It can give you the feeling that you're part of an elite, someone at the cutting edge of whatever topic is under discussion. We hesitate to give examples because it's such an ephemeral phenomenon, with new words and expressions constantly appearing to create new meanings and concepts. By the time this book is published, any examples we'd offered would probably have vanished or would sound embarrassingly old-fashioned. The problem is that, while some of these terms are useful and encapsulate a particular part of the *Zeitgeist*, many are lazy approximations. People use them instead of bothering to articulate a precise thought. They give a spurious impression of authenticity when, frequently, they're rather a cloak for ignorance. As George Orwell wrote:

> The great enemy of clear language is insincerity. When there is a gap between one's real and one's declared aims, one turns as it were instinctively to long words and exhausted idioms, like a cuttlefish squirting out ink.

> (Orwell, 1946)

Having said all that, however, we must acknowledge that there's another type of 'jargon' that you do need to master. In fact, jargon isn't really the right word because what we're referring to is the fact that almost all academic subjects do have their own terminology. Whatever your discipline, it will have terms, expressions and conventions that convey exact concepts for which there are no substitutes. You'll keep on coming across them in the specialist books and articles you read, and you must make them part of your own, natural academic vocabulary. But make sure you know what they mean and, if you're not confident that the word you've chosen is the right one, find an alternative. Faced with a choice between an unfamiliar word and one which is simpler but of whose meaning you're certain, choose simplicity.

Using the ideas of others

Many assignments may include a significant number of quotations and citations. The way in which you incorporate them into your writing will influence the power of your arguments and the overall readability of your work. If, for example, you were writing an essay on the nature of language, you wouldn't get many marks for:

> Thomas Carlyle said that: 'Language is called the garment of thought: however, it should rather be, language is the flesh-garment, the body, of thought.' Wittgenstein had the same idea. He said: 'The limits of my language mean the limits of my world.' The Theatre of the Absurd was concerned with language, too. The critic, Irving Wardle, said that it used: 'An iron precision of language and construction as the writer's only defence against the chaos of living experience.'[2]

The quotations are well-chosen but badly used. The writer is trying to let them do all the work. Rather than create his own argument and use them to reinforce and support it, he's stringing them together in the hope that their precision and aptness will make his point. The trouble is that we, the readers, don't know what his point is. We know what Carlyle, Wittgenstein and Wardle thought, but the writer of the essay seems simply to be acting as their secretary.

On top of that, consider the stylistic effect of that example. As well as failing to expand, or even comment, on the quotations, the writer's simply tacked them onto one another so that the reader lurches from point to point with no easy transition. The short paragraph is made up

---

2 Another problem with this passage is that, by failing to identify the source of the various quotations, we've laid ourselves open to a charge of plagiarism. Even though the different authors have been named and their words have been enclosed within quotation marks, the impression left by multiplying extracts from elsewhere is simply that we're borrowing someone else's ideas. ALWAYS identify your sources fully.

of three separate lumps of text. There's no topic sentence, no development, no termination or transition – in fact, no sense at all of a strong, unified argument.

It wouldn't take much to improve it and, while our intention in this book is to avoid suggesting that there is one 'correct' way to write and, equally, to avoid providing models for you to copy, a reworking of the extract will help to show what we mean. So, one way (among many), of using the same material might be as follows:

> Writers and philosophers have always been fascinated by the relationship between language and reality. In the nineteenth century, Thomas Carlyle (2001: 123) wrote that, rather than calling language 'the garment of thought', it should be seen as 'the flesh-garment, the body, of thought'. In simpler terms, he was suggesting that words do not simply describe ideas, they are themselves the ideas, a notion reinforced in the twentieth century by Wittgenstein (2006: 68), when he wrote, 'The limits of my language mean the limits of my world'. In the troubled years after the Second World War, the same belief that language defined reality was demonstrated by the writers of the Theatre of the Absurd who, according to the critic, Irving Wardle (1968: 14–15), used 'An iron precision of language and construction as [their] only defence against the chaos of living experience'.

It's a longer paragraph and we're making no great claims as to its quality, but it does contain more substance. The three quotations are linked, made to relate to one another, and the language/reality relationship is stressed. Most important of all, the quotations are supporting the writer's ideas, not being used as substitutes for them. Once again, it's a matter of taking care with the transitions between points. Don't just make sure you choose the right linking expression ('because', 'as a result', 'on the other hand', and so on), but expand the substance of the quotation, give it a wider context, develop it. Think of your separate notes, ideas and quotations as organic constructions that grow into one another.

Be careful not to over-use quotations, however well chosen and appropriate they seem. If you're relying all the time on other people's words, there's bound to be an unevenness of style and the reader will be left wondering where you are in amongst them all. There are times when it's necessary to use the actual words of your source but there are many others when a summary of the ideas would be just as effective.

Introducing and formatting quotations

You'll notice how we formatted the two extracts above differently from the main body of our text. They weren't 'quotations' as such, but they were separate from our main argument and used as illustrations of a particular point. When you use direct quotations, the conventions are simple. If you're quoting more than thirty words, you should usually separate the quotation from the body of your work, indent it on both sides, and use single line spacing. You don't need to use inverted commas. The source information (author, date and page number), should be enclosed in brackets after the quotation.

QR

Quotations
and
citations

If it's shorter than thirty words, keep it as part of your normal formatting but show that it's a quotation by enclosing it within inverted commas. Be careful how you introduce it and make sure that, when you read it, it flows evenly from and into the words around it.

Plagiarism

Plagiarism has always been a problem and, with even wider access to original materials now available online, it's a source of serious concern. Plagiarism is theft. It may seem a quick-fix answer for someone who's under pressure to hand in an assignment but those who take that route are deceiving themselves. They're selling themselves short by accepting marks that belong to someone else. In the end, plagiarizing is losing.

Sometimes, the impulse to plagiarize is easy to understand. It may be that you labour away trying to get to grips with a problem and, suddenly, you come across an academic article or a chapter in a book that seems to express exactly what you've been groping towards. The temptation then is to restate its findings, either using the same words or trying to hide them in some sort of paraphrase, without identifying where they came from or to whom they belonged.

Another problem may be that the subject is so popular that you find many books and articles on it, lots of which say the same things, and you feel that there's nothing new to be said by a 'mere' student like yourself. It's a problem we all face. This book, for example, has some observations and suggestions similar (or maybe even identical), to those you'll probably find in many other 'how to write an essay' books. That's not because we've stolen them, it's because there are some basic, common-sense approaches that we and many other teachers and writers have learned through actually reading and marking students' essays and writing articles and books ourselves. They're our own ideas, but many of them are shared by thousands of others. However, if we had quoted anyone else's work directly, or taken ideas and/or examples from them without acknowledging where we'd got them, that would be plagiarism and it would undermine, if not destroy, our own credibility and the book's value.

There's also the issue of unconscious plagiarism. You may have a flash of inspiration and come up with what you think is an original idea. If it is, congratulations, but check it out first. It's quite common for people to forget the original source of an idea and just assume that it's their own. Perhaps you're simply seeing an old idea in a different context, or it was in something you read a long time ago. So, when you get those 'eureka' moments, it's worth thinking carefully about possible sources that you may have forgotten about. Ask others (such as your tutor or supervisor), whether they've come across the idea before, look up relevant texts, encyclopaedias or search the Internet. Even if you're not aware of the fact that you're using someone else's work, it's still plagiarism.

Using the words and ideas of others is a legitimate part of academic research and learning generally, but you must always acknowledge your sources. If you don't, the grades you're awarded are meaningless and, if the plagiarism is discovered, it could seriously affect your chances of even getting a degree.[3]

Summarizing someone else's arguments

One way of using source material is to summarize it. It's still essential to identify your source but, by putting it into words you've chosen yourself, you can give it a particular, personal emphasis, adapt it to suit the specific argument you're developing. If you use a direct quotation, the words are obviously those of someone else, but summarizing them lets you incorporate them more easily into your own thinking.

First, let's be clear what a summary is. It's condensed from all or part of the source material, written in your own words, and it stays faithful to the sense and ideas of the original author. You must keep your own opinions on the ideas separate from it and, as ever, you must clearly identify where and from whom the ideas originated.

---

3 It's never worth the risk. Today's technology makes the detection of plagiarism very easy.

Summarizing doesn't just mean paraphrasing another person's work by taking his or her key phrases and rearranging them; you must understand the ideas they're expressing and reword them. That means reading the text to familiarize yourself with the content and then reading it again to get a deeper understanding of its ideas. During this second reading, it's useful to label each section of the work, or each idea, using a general term, preferably a word that isn't in the actual text. Now write the labels down as a list, then read through the text again and, when you've finished, turn it over or put it aside and, alongside each label, write down in your own words the ideas it refers to. It's a way of getting more familiar and comfortable with the ideas and refining them in your own words and style.

When you write the actual summary, use your own notes, not the source material BUT always use the author's name to attribute the ideas to the source; for example, 'Weyers (2006) states that . . .' or, if the source isn't contemporary, use the past tense, 'Adamson (1998) claimed that . . .' Now read the summary critically, checking that it identifies the key ideas of the original and explains them using new words and terminology. If you can cut it down, do so, because you want to be as concise and as easy to read as possible.

DIY

Rewording
quotations

One final point on this subject: sometimes, a summary may be so short that it hardly seems to be a summary at all. For example, you may write: 'It is possible that the hydroxy group on the third carbon has its origin in the ester conjugate (Smith, 1996), but recent findings suggest that . . .'. The statement you're making isn't a summary but the reference in brackets indicates that you're basing it on the ideas that can be found in Smith's article.

But, whether you're quoting, summarizing or simply referring to someone else's material, always identify the person and the source.[4]

The introduction

Usually, an academic assignment consists of three major sections: introduction, main argument, and conclusion but, as we keep reminding you, there's no single 'correct' way to organize and write it. Our approach has been putting all the emphasis on the main argument and we'd even go so far as to say that it makes more sense to write that

---

4 The QRs on pp. 130–2 and 155–9 remind you of some of the basics of this process.

before you write the introduction. It's the main body that presents the information, the argument and the key points of your response to the assignment, so your attention should be focused on making that as full and clear as possible. If you write an introduction first, you may set goals that you find it difficult to attain, so you're placing restrictions on your approach. In crude terms, we could ask in this context 'How do you know where you're going until you've been there?' It's entirely up to you, of course, but our preferred option is to leave writing the introduction and conclusion until last.

We've stressed the desirability and usefulness of organizing your notes before you start writing, but it's a fact that the very act of writing and developing your ideas may change your approach. Writing is a flexible, evolving process and, as you write, new ideas may occur, the previous ones may seem less persuasive, and you may want to change the sequence of your arguments. That's fine. It all comes from a deeper understanding of your material. Your organized note sequence is still your path through the assignment, but you can be flexible with it, adapt it to take different directions. As long as you prepared it conscientiously to begin with, there's no danger of getting completely lost. Then, when you've finished that first draft, you can be confident that you know what you're introducing.

Different topics and disciplines call for different introductions, so it's best for you to find out what your department prefers. In general terms, however, we can identify the general areas that might be covered. They include:

- giving some general background information on the broad subject area and more detailed information on the specific topic you're writing about;
- explaining your understanding and interpretation of the terms used in the assignment;
- outlining the parameters of your answer;
- saying how you intend to tackle the assignment.

The introduction and conclusion are closely linked. By indicating at the outset that you intend to follow a particular path, you're anticipating some of the things you'll be saying at the end of the assignment. For that reason, it's perhaps worth using fairly broad strokes to sketch your intentions at this stage. Then, when you've written the conclusion, you can return to the introduction and sharpen the details to make sure that they coincide with your actual findings.

By the way, people often think that you should start your essay with a sentence or piece of writing that grabs the reader's attention. This may be true of some sorts of creative writing, but it doesn't necessarily apply to academic writing. Be clear, be interesting, but avoid gimmicks.

The conclusion

The conclusion should revisit the points covered in the main body of the work and show that you've achieved the aim you stated in your introduction. The skill you use in summarizing your material at this point will reveal how good you are at analytical and critical thinking. It's also the last section markers will read to remind them of what's in the rest of the piece. So it's worth taking some trouble over it.

This is where your mini-conclusions will come in useful by reminding you of your key points. By pulling them quickly together in your conclusion, you'll be able to give your reader a very clear reminder of the road you've travelled and your final position on the matter under discussion.

Once again, we're not offering rules, but guidelines so, in your conclusion, you might:

- revisit the background information on the broad subject area and the key issues of the topic itself;
- reiterate how you've interpreted the question;
- show that you've tackled the question in the way your introduction said you would;
- restate a viewpoint or opinion you've reached, presented, supported or refuted;
- and, perhaps, indicate any further work that might be done on the issue or further questions that have been raised;
- finally, make sure that it fits with what you wrote in your introduction.

Writer's block

Writer's block is simply a temporary inability to write. It can happen to anyone. Even seasoned writers do, at some stage, experience the symptoms. Your mind goes blank, your brain's numb or you're just totally void of ideas. The condition doesn't usually last long, but it's a problem if there's a deadline looming. So, if it strikes, what can you do?

First of all, don't panic – that'll make it worse. Start to think logically about what you're trying to do and then try some strategies to overcome the block. There are various tricks that have been suggested by writers who've been through the process themselves. We offer some here as quick suggestions that you can try or adapt to your particular needs:

- It helps to think positively. You know you can write this sort of thing. You've done it before.
- Change the physical way you're writing. If you're at the keyboard, use a pen instead, or vice versa.
- Read over what you've written already. Note down any ideas that come into your mind as you read. These could be starting points when you get back to your pen or keyboard. Or the simple process of writing down something could start to remove the block.
- Write about something totally unrelated to the assignment, even complete 'stream of consciousness' rubbish. By making your 'writing muscles' work without engaging your 'thinking muscles' you'll be moving towards being unblocked.
- Explain your ideas on the topic to someone else, or talk out loud to yourself.
- Alternatively, relax and do something totally different – clean up your room, do the dishes, go for a walk, play some music. Switching your attention away from the writing may be enough to do the trick.

One of the factors that will help you through the problem is the assurance that your organized material is there to keep leading you through the process of composition. The problem may still arise but, if it does, remember that it's temporary. Try the techniques we've suggested. There's no single way that works for everyone and you may find one completely unrelated to the ones we've listed. But you will find one.

Word processing

From the start, the suggestions we've made seem to have assumed that your work is paper-based, that your notes are written in longhand and that, when you're organizing your material, the process involves sorting through pieces of paper. Nowadays, more and more people prefer to work directly on the screen using a word-processing programme. If you do, you'll find the techniques we're proposing are perhaps even easier to apply.

When you're collecting your material, for example, it's easy to save it all into a single file. Let's call it *mainfile.doc*. When you have everything you need, work your way through the file, sorting the material into groups under sub-headings or, if you prefer, cut notes and paste them into new files. If we use the colour image we proposed in Chapter 4, that would mean that you're gradually emptying *mainfile.doc* and filling various new files called *red.doc*, *blue.doc* and so on. When the main file's completely empty, take each of the other files in turn and rearrange the notes they contain, by cutting and pasting them, to form the coherent sequence of your argument. As we've said, it's exactly the same process as with individual notes on pieces of paper, and it's easy to try out various combinations to see what gives you the best flow. The last action before starting to write is to paste the different smaller documents back into the main file in the 'correct' sequence so that you now have a *mainfile.doc* that carries your organized material.

Now you can either work on the main file and move through it, linking the points as we've described above, or copy sequences from it, paste them into a temporary file (perhaps *temp.doc*) and concentrate on blending them into a smooth argument before putting them back into the main document.

There's no doubt that word processing saves a lot of time and effort. Its advantages seem clear:

- it's convenient and can be time-saving when you're writing and editing;
- its flexibility lets you move around and insert text wherever you like;
- print-outs are legible and, if it's approved of by your department, you can use different fonts, headings or spacing to group or emphasize points;
- it's easier to import charts, tables, computer graphics and images; and
- it has various useful tools such as spelling and grammar checkers, a thesaurus, a word count facility.

BUT . . .

- Spell checkers aren't foolproof. They can't look at a word's context. When they see the word 'form', they think it's OK, even in the sentence 'Shakespeare came form Stratford'.
- They don't know the difference between homophones such as 'their' and 'there'.

- If you're not careful with setting the language, they accept American spellings such as 'color' instead of 'colour'.

Also, it's sometimes tempting to experiment with functions just because they're there, to produce fancy fonts and striking formatting. This can easily give the impression that you're valuing visual style over actual substance. If your argument's clear and strong, wrapping it in gimmicks will serve only to weaken it. And, anyway, tinkering with formatting will take time that would be better spent thinking about and writing the assignment. As with everything else we've been discussing, the tools that you're using to create your text should aim to give your thinking its clearest possible expression and make it easier to read.

QR

Word-processing tips

DIY TASK 1

Structuring paragraphs

The following paragraphs are based on adequate, coherent examples of well-developed arguments, but the sentences they contain have been altered slightly and rearranged to undermine each paragraph's overall structure. Try to rearrange them and change a few words here and there so that, once again, their ideas flow smoothly and logically from a topic sentence to a terminator sentence:

- Jane Austen seemed to take pleasure in the activities of her characters. She failed to extend the same degree of tolerance towards her neighbours. D. H. Lawrence considered her to be 'mean'. Her letters are often cruel, even spiteful. Other critics have variously pointed to the fact that her main response to those of whom she did not approve was one of disdain. Is a person whose attitudes are conditioned by her personal likes and dislikes capable of the objectivity necessary for passing judgements on her fellows? They leave few reputations unchallenged. Is her subjectivity a prism that gives her focus an added intensity? What does this reveal about the nature of the social criticism for which she is so justly praised?

- Writers use language to expose the hypocrisy of politicians. The fact that they see themselves as having a higher goal still does not separate them from those they seek to criticize. It would seem, therefore, that words are dangerous, whoever is using them. Language is a very powerful tool. Politicians use language to manipulate people. But the writer is just as guilty of manipulation. He claims that his aims are those of society. He has an agenda, he shapes his words to create a specific effect and, as a result, he is responsible for distorting the vision of his reader. The politicians say exactly the same thing. Propaganda is seen by some as a necessary evil but by others as just lies.

- Those who appreciate the sharpness of Kenneth Tynan or the measured gravity of Harold Hobson will point to the fact that their influence on theatre exceeded that of many dramatists. The appreciation and explication of a text's subtleties demands a precise control of language. The dramatist makes his living as a wordsmith and should be judged by his peers. However, if critics were indeed his peers, would they not be dramatists instead? The fact remains that, without the dramatists, they would have nothing to write about. Literary criticism exists at a lower level than the texts it examines.

DIY TASK 2

Rewording quotations

A useful exercise would be for you to take a few quotations now
and turn them into your own words.

We could invent some for the purpose but it would obviously be
more useful for you to be dealing with a style and terminology
appropriate to your own discipline.

The suggestion, therefore, is that you find a few examples in some
relevant articles or text books and practise rewording them as if
you were using them in an assignment.

You could use the appropriate reporting words in the DIY task
on p. 50 to introduce them.

Chapter 6

Style and impact

What is writing style?

For many people, the word 'style', when applied to writing, evokes notions of elevated expressions, fancy words, panache. The assumption is that to do something 'with style' is to add a special dimension or an extra layer to it. That's fine and it's certainly one of the familiar meanings of the word. A more basic, less loaded meaning, however, is that 'style' simply refers to the way something is expressed. '♥U' and 'I love you' say the same thing, but in different ways. Emails, text messages, letters, CVs, minutes of meetings , novels, essays – all have distinct, recognizable forms, which are often far from elevated.

'Back in 5 mins', 'Dinner in oven', 'Bus late' are all examples of quick notes that eschew grammatical correctness but convey their information in a clear, concise and appropriate manner. It's difficult, though, to imagine even a casual conversation being conducted in the same style. And, speaking of conversation, consider this familiar exchange:

> 'How are you?'
> 'Fine thanks. You?'
> 'Fine.'
> 'Good.'

There's nothing 'wrong' with it, but rather than a record of two individuals expressing curiosity about one another's health, it's an example of phatic communication; in other words, speech that conveys not information, but sociability.

Style, then, is a combination of distinctive words and verbal structures that characterize a particular person, group, activity or context. So what are the words and structures that define academic writing?

Well, if it was that easy, we'd simply give you a list of guidelines and there'd be no need to write a whole chapter about it. Academic writing encompasses many different forms, from letters to oral presentations, scientific reports to essays on Fine Arts. The style for each is different and, while there are certain agreed conventions, there are still debates about the permissible balance between such things as formality and informality, objectivity and subjectivity, passive and active constructions. Most of the conventions are addressed in the most popular guides to academic methods and styles that we've already mentioned: the Chicago, Vancouver, Harvard and MLA style sheets.[1] We'll look at some of the debates and conventions in Chapter 7 but in this chapter, our focus will be on more general effects and the components you'll be using to create your own academic style – words, sentences, paragraphs. The intention is to help you not only to articulate your ideas clearly but also to give them greater impact.

First, we should stress that we won't be offering a model for you to imitate. The problem with trying to reproduce a particular style or a specific terminology is that you can end up just imitating the surface features of a discipline instead of getting inside its way of thinking. Having said that, however, we don't underestimate the value of being aware of how writers achieve their effects. If you're impressed by a book or an article, or it seems to be making its points particularly clearly, have a look at the author's technique and use what you learn from that to improve your own style.

What and who?

In Chapter 1 we proposed ways of approaching the assignment. They can be reduced to two sets of questions:

- First, what are you being asked to do? What's the instruction word (or words) in your title? Does the marker want information? Analysis? Brevity? A tight focus? A broad approach? Speculation? Facts?
- Next, who are you writing it for? What do they want to hear? How do they want to hear it? What effect are you trying to create for them? How would you like them to respond?

---

1 See p. 33 and the QR on Bibliographies and reference lists: pp. 130–2.

All writing is selection. It's a form of shorthand, an exercise that confronts the complexity of thought and arranges it in a set of constructions for the reader to interpret. The better the writing, the easier it is to understand. In a way, the process can be seen as a pact between writer and reader, an artificial way of making thoughts and abstractions accessible.[2]

It's easier to explain if we take the example of fiction. A novelist writes, 'She picked up her coat and walked to the door' and the reader accepts the reality of the event. But consider how much more complex that reality is. Which hand did she use to pick up the coat? Did she have to reach for it? Did she walk slowly or quickly? With long strides or short steps? Did she limp? What was the initial trigger for the whole sequence – a decision on her part, or the firing of synapses in her brain, the action of enzymes, the conversion of nutrients within her digestive system, the transportation of oxygen to the relevant parts of her body, the contraction of a muscle? Clearly, the series of causes and effects that combined to constitute the 'reality' runs into millions. A 'full' description of every process and event that contributed to that one, simple scene would fill many volumes, and yet the writer achieves the desired effect by selecting just two actions. It's a trivial example of the complicity between writer and reader, but it may help you to understand the need to make that complicity easy for the person who'll be reading your work.

The aim then, is to interest and inform the reader and this can be achieved in some surprising ways. For example, just the look of the text on the page could be important. Many of you will have had the experience of opening a book or journal and being confronted with solid blocks of text on each page, with few indentations or other paragraph markers to indicate a point at which you could pause. In a way, it implies that there's going to be a relentlessness about the content, a drive that gives little room for reflection. It may be a false perception, but the psychological effect of such an experience, however careful you are to suppress it, could be to trigger a 'boredom warning' response or predispose you against the person responsible for the text you're reading.

So, does this mean that there should be several paragraphs per page? And, if so, how many?

---

2 We've referred to this writer–reader collaboration many times. It's central to the whole process of writing.

Once again, that's not the way it works. There's no optimum length for a paragraph. We've already discussed how they're structured in Chapter 5 and, since each is a unit of thought devoted to developing one main idea, their length will depend on the nature and complexity of that idea. So, if that's the case, how can you avoid the 'monster paragraph' syndrome?

Well, one way is to use the technique we suggested in Chapter 5 of reducing each paragraph to a bullet point. If you find that you need more than one bullet point to convey the meaning, perhaps the paragraph could be divided. Equally, if you have a few very short paragraphs, check how close the bullet points are to one another in terms of meaning and think about whether they could be combined to form a longer paragraph. And, if the short paragraphs are all very different, could some or all of them be expanded by adding details to develop them more fully?

DIY

Paragraph sequencing

There's no rule that says you must have *x* paragraphs to a page but remember the 'boredom warning' response and try to mix yours up in terms of length to give your readers variety and sustain their interest.

Sentence structure

As we've said, putting a thought into words clarifies it. You may think you know what you mean until you try to write it down and find that it's elusive. Here, though, we're concerned not just with pinning down the idea but with giving it a specific slant, strengthening its impact. If you like, we want to achieve both meaning and persuasion.

Let's start with a couple of simple constructions. There are no grammatical or other 'mistakes' in either of them, their content is more or less the same, and yet each provokes a different response in the reader because of the way in which they're expressed and organized; in other words, their style:

> Isaac Newton's father, who died in October 1642, three months before the birth of his son, was a farmer who owned property and animals, which made him a wealthy man, but he was completely uneducated and could not sign his own name.

> Isaac Newton's father, a wealthy, property-owning farmer, was uneducated and could not sign his own name. He died in October 1642, three months before his son was born.

Why do you think there's a difference? Is it the actual words used, the sequencing of the information, the length of the sentences, the punctuation, or some other aspect of the writing? Take a few moments to look at them and decide for yourself.

Sentences can be complex constructions but, for the purposes of our argument, we're going to simplify their components. As far as possible, we'll try to avoid using labels and expressions such as 'subordination', 'defining and non-defining relative clauses', and 'floating participles' and instead focus on the relative 'importance' of the different parts of the sentence.[3]

Let's take another example:

> Cromwell was radicalized by his strong religious faith which started with his conversion – the result of an experience he had some time before the Civil War – and was strengthened by a belief that he and his troops had been chosen by God to fight the good fight. This also conditioned his political actions during the Protectorate.

There is no single 'correct' way of transmitting all the information contained in the two sentences, but let's begin by dividing it into fragments:

1 Cromwell was radicalized by his strong religious faith
2 which started with his conversion
3 the result of an experience he had
4 some time before the Civil War
5 and was strengthened by a belief that he and his troops had been chosen by God
6 to fight the good fight
7 This also conditioned his political actions
8 during the Protectorate.

So, in our reading of the text, we've identified eight separate pieces of information. It's easy to see that the most important piece is the

---

3 The writing of this sentence itself illustrated the need for careful word selection. The first draft ended '. . . to focus on those parts of the sentence that are more or less important'. This created a problem: we meant 'more important and less important parts' but if you'd read 'more or less' to mean 'approximately', our meaning would have been lost.

first. Everything else, including the second sentence (7 + 8) depends on, explains or expands it. In stylistic terms, the effect of presenting the information in this form is to move from strength to weakness. The sentence opens with a strong statement but then adds more and more bits of (relatively less important) information, which progressively dilutes the initial effect. The final (important) assertion – that his political policies were also conditioned by his faith – reads almost as an afterthought and is lost in the extended list. We're not suggesting that all long sentences are bad, but it's true that how you place fragments of information in relation to others does affect their impact.[4]

The opening and closing sections of a sentence are usually more emphatic than the middle sections. It's also true that, if a sentence is made up of many elements, the main clause (number 1 in our example) has more prominence than the others. So it's easy to see that, if you want to emphasize something, you should put it at the end or the beginning of a sentence and, if a piece of information is important, it shouldn't be hidden in a subordinate clause. If we apply these observations to our example and rewrite it accordingly, one of the possible versions of it might be:

> Before the Civil War, Cromwell had an experience which led to a religious conversion. The strength of his faith, increased by a belief that he and his troops had been chosen by God, radicalized him and, during the Protectorate, conditioned his political actions.

It still conveys all the necessary information, but places the emphasis on the more important points. If we break it down as before, we get:

1   Before the Civil War (weak)[5]
2   Cromwell had an experience which led to a religious conversion (strong)
3   The strength of his faith . . . radicalized him (strong)

---

4 There are other stylistic points to note here. The expression 'some time before', for example, is imprecise and suggests inadequate research, while the cliché 'to fight the good fight' undermines the power implicit in being 'chosen by God' and, placed as it is at the end of the sentence (a 'strong' position), is an example of bathos (anticlimax). Finally, it's by no means clear what 'This', in fragment 7, refers to because it's preceded by so many possibilities.
5 The words 'weak' and 'strong' here refer not to the content of the selected text but to the relative impact it has as a result of its placing in the sentence.

4   increased by a belief that he and his troops had been chosen by God (weak)
5   and, during the Protectorate (weak)
6   conditioned his political actions (strong).

So, when you're editing and you come across a passage that seems unsatisfactory, try moving its elements around. Identify the parts of your message you want to stress and place them accordingly, and be aware of the negative effect of a sentence that ends with a generalization. Note, for example, how the following sentence starts with some powerful points but dribbles weakly away in the last few words:

> Cromwell's religious fervour drove him to reform the legal, judicial and social systems of England and abolish immorality, drunkenness and other activities.

The same effect is created if you use expressions such as 'etc.' or 'and so on'. The writer of the next example seems to be in confident control of her material until the final word lets her down:

> All plant cells depend on cytoplasmic streaming in eukaryotic cells to help with the delivery of nutrients, metabolites, etc.

'Etc.' here can mean different things, none of them encouraging:

- the list of 'deliverables' is too long to quote in full;
  - the writer's too lazy to think of any more;
  - the writer's not sure which other ones there are, if any.

DIY

Structuring
sentences

Whatever the reason, its effect on the reader is to weaken the impact of the sentence and, perhaps, suggest that the writer hasn't done enough research. The same is true if we replace 'etc.' with expressions such as 'and so on' or 'and other things'.[6] The easiest way to avoid that particular pitfall is to do what we've just done and use 'such as'. The above example would then end with 'the delivery of substances such as nutrients and

---

6 By the way, we're aware of the fact that we've used the expression 'and so on' in the course of writing this book. As we said at the outset, however, the style we're adopting is close to a conversational one and not an example of academic writing.

metabolites'. It gives the impression that you've chosen two examples from what could be a much longer list.

For sentences, as for paragraphs, length is not an issue. Long sentences are not inherently more or less important than short ones. They do, however, run the risk of obscuring the central point if it's surrounded by too many layers. If, when you're editing, you come across a sentence that stretches beyond perhaps four lines, check it carefully, just to make sure that its meaning is still clear. If it isn't, or if you're unsure about it, it's safer to rewrite it as two separate sentences.

But beware the metronome effect. By that, we mean the effect created by a series of sentences that are all of more or less the same length. The reader becomes aware that the information is being conveyed in regular lumps and it's difficult for her to appreciate the overall flow of the argument. Reading the following example will show you what we mean:

DIY

Sentences that are too long

> In its early phases, quantum theory applied to Euclidean space. It used Cartesian tensors of linear and angular momentum. Quantum theory moved on when Einstein read a paper written by Bose. He realized it was important. In the paper, Bose proposed different states for the photon. Einstein made sure that the paper was published.

The sensation is one of being fed discrete, self-contained fragments of material. It's obvious that they're linked with one another because they're about the same things – 'Einstein', 'quantum theory', 'paper' – but we have to work hard to fit them together. It takes very little effort to vary the effect by altering the length of the sentences, joining some together with simple constructions, and revealing the information progressively rather than jumping back and forward as in the original:

> In its early phases, quantum theory applied to Euclidean space and used Cartesian tensors of linear and angular momentum. It moved on when Einstein read a paper written by Bose, in which different states for the photon were proposed. Recognizing its importance, Einstein ensured its publication.

Notice, too, how the last sentence, made up of two short pieces of information, is as effective as those which precede it. So, as we said, the length of sentences isn't important in itself, as long as you avoid creating the metronomic effect. In fact, you can make length work to your advantage. If, for example, you want to emphasize a particular point, you might convey it in a short sentence that comes at the end of a sequence of longer ones, or even just one long one, as in this example:

> It has been argued that the power of the philosophical stance of the Romantic generation derived from the need to respond positively to the experience of void generated by the upheavals and uncertainties of its historical moment, and build solid structures and a purposeful identity to bridge the emptiness. The reverse was true; identity was itself defined by the void.

DIY

Overcoming the metronome effect

As with paragraphs, think of your sentences as organic structures that grow into and out of one another, linking closely to lead the reader seamlessly through your arguments.

Expand your word power

To create sentences, you need words. Of course, you'll need the specialized terminology of your own field, which you'll find in discipline-specific dictionaries or perhaps in glossaries in textbooks. But you'll also need a wider general vocabulary. When we wrote earlier about 'notes that eschew grammatical correctness', we weren't trying to impress you with the word 'eschew'; it was a word that said exactly what we meant. Think about it. If you agree that writing down an idea defines it and makes it clearer, it follows that the more words you have at your disposal, the more precise your ideas can be, and the subtler the distinctions you can make between them. Equally, if you accept the notion that sentences should be treated as organic structures that you have to fuse to sustain your flow, the more varied and flexible the elements that make up those structures, the easier it'll be to find ways of linking them.

A quick (but not necessarily easy) way of accessing more words is to use a dictionary of synonyms or a thesaurus. Most word-processing programmes have a thesaurus facility although they tend not to offer as many alternatives as those published in book form. The process is simple; you look up a word and find a list of other words and expressions that have a similar meaning. But there's a problem – they don't actually tell you the meaning of each alternative. Let's say you write the sentence 'Careful scrutiny of the data revealed that . . .' but you realize that you've already used 'careful' in the previous sentence. You want an alternative, so you look up 'careful' in a thesaurus – and you find several alternatives, from 'circumspect' to 'vigilant', 'painstaking' to 'punctilious', 'scrupulous' to 'finical'. If you see one whose meaning you're sure of and which is right for the context, fine. If not, check with a dictionary.

DIY

Avoiding repetitions

Another type of reference work that can help you to increase and/or refine your vocabulary is a collocation dictionary. In fact, some linguists claim that it's even more useful than a thesaurus. In simple terms, collocations are words or phrases that naturally go together to form a familiar expression, which then exists as a separate 'meaning' in its own right. The words 'crystal' and 'clear', for example, are both useable in a variety of contexts. Put them together, though, and they create a new concept – 'crystal clear'.

Sometimes, the collocation can mean something quite distinct from the literal meaning of the words that combine to create it. Someone who's ready and eager to get going, for example, is often said to be 'bright-eyed and bushy-tailed', a description which, to anyone unfamiliar with that particular usage, would be anatomically disturbing. The simple word 'bank' has totally different meanings when collocated with 'river' and 'piggy'. And the expression 'ladies and gentlemen of the press' conveys an impression of something other than the refined good manners normally associated with the opening three words of the phrase.

Collocations are 'part and parcel' of everyday language, extending its possibilities and providing writers and speakers with extra effects and stylistic variations.

One final point: the best way of expanding your vocabulary is to read – not just textbooks and articles, but newspapers, books, pamphlets, journals, everything. When we were discussing gathering material for your assignment, we encouraged you to restrict your reading to texts that were central to your topic, but true education, the real ability to handle ideas and to develop your thinking, calls for exposure to the many styles and complexities of language. Reading is writing is thinking.

DIY TASK 1

Paragraph sequencing

Select a page from a book or article or, best of all, from a piece of work you've written yourself and try to reduce each separate paragraph to a bullet point. If you need more than one bullet point, try dividing the relevant paragraph into smaller paragraphs so that each can be represented. Then put the original text aside and read through the bullet points to see the flow of ideas. Look for repetitions and gaps, see where the argument builds to make its point and look for any anti-climactic effects. If you're using a piece of your own work, it should help you to see very quickly how moving paragraphs around, deleting some, combining others can improve the overall flow.

DIY TASK 2

Structuring sentences

In this chapter, we've given examples of how moving elements around in a sentence can strengthen it and increase its impact. Here are some more examples of poorly constructed sentences for you to improve:

- The research possibilities offered by enzymes far exceed those associated with cell surface receptors, nuclear hormone receptors, ion channels, etc.

- The Amphibian Age was the Permian period, which is so designated because rocks from this period were first identified in the Perm Province in northeast Russia. It lasted 32 million years and ended 248 million years ago, when the Earth's atmosphere reached the same oxygen levels as it has today. The Mesozoic era began when the Permian period ended with the largest ever mass extinction, the cause of which is unknown, but in the early part of the period the dominant species were the labyrinthodonts.

- The revolution in perception brought about by Manet came not from a mere change of palette but of a deconstruction of light itself, examples of which are to be found in almost all his open air subjects.

- The French Revolution ended on November 10, 1799, when the *Directoire*, which had taken over from the *Convention* on November 2, 1795, was replaced by the Consulate, which led eventually to the First Empire.

DIY TASK 3

Sentences that are too long

The following examples show how difficult it is to sustain meaning through a sentence that piles extra pieces of information one on top of another. Rewrite them as two or more sentences in each case to make the text more interesting and give the various points greater impact:

- Advanced methods for determining the dynamics of receptor cells have begun to make it possible for researchers to design drugs effectively without having to subject them to the usual series of random tests and sustained monitoring procedures which were previously necessary to establish the specific processes which guaranteed the drug's viability and validated the documentation which would need to accompany it when it was forwarded for consideration by the relevant committee.

- 347 of the drugs prescribed in the period under review work by inhibiting one or more of 71 enzymes, only 48 of which are human, according to a team of biochemists who analysed official government records and categorized them to provide statistically significant data on which companies could base their marketing strategies.

- When Camus claims that the human condition is ideally represented by the figure of Sisyphus, he has necessarily to exclude the narrative element that insists that the task of rolling the rock up the hill is a punishment and therefore the consequence of the actions of some force superior to Sisyphus himself, a moral force whose pre-eminence is founded on codes which permit judgements to be made against criteria deriving from a higher existential plane and therefore posits a dimension in which salvation is possible.

DIY TASK 4

Overcoming the metronome effect

Here are two paragraphs that, once again, have been very badly written to illustrate the deadening effect of metronomic regularity. All the sentences are of a similar length. Your task is to rewrite them and fuse sentences to produce a more fluid, more readable piece of text. You may find that the first needs to be divided into more than one paragraph. The second consists almost entirely of terms that will be unfamiliar to non-specialists but it would still be valuable for you to try to improve it. Your focus will be on linguistic, not medical factors:

- There are many inter-relationships between different macro-economic variables. The relationship between interest rates and the exchange rate comes into play when bank rates rise. These fluctuations indicate that the relevant country's economy is growing stronger. When unemployment is high, however, growth rates tend to be depressed. Poor retail figures and a slowdown in the housing market also tend to slow growth. Any rise in interest rates tends to help control inflationary pressures. It also has an impact on traders operating in the currency markets. Exchange rates will move up and down as the news about interest rates is broadcast. The more shrewd speculators complete their trades before this effect is felt. Exporters, too, are affected by these fluctuations. As dollars, pounds and euros move against one another, their products become competitive. Exports appear more expensive and consequently there is less demand for them. The trend is in the opposite direction for tourists, who get more foreign currency for their money. Their spending power at their destination is correspondingly greater. There are constant reminders of the importance of macro-economic interdependence. They demonstrate how difficult it is for policy makers to control inflation and stimulate growth at the same time.

- Endocytosis is the cellular uptake of macromolecules and particulate substances by localized regions of the plasma membrane. These regions surround the substance and form an intracellular vesicle. There are several steps in endocytosis, including membrane budding to form vesicles. These vesicles are transported to a particular target. There they dock and fuse with destination membranes. Endocytosis plays an important role in transcellular transport and immune responses. It is also important in signal transduction, neural function and many pathological conditions.

DIY TASK 5

Avoiding repetitions

For this task, the poor writing is the result of word repetitions. Rewrite the paragraph. It may be helpful to consult a thesaurus to find alternative words or expressions:

- The debate between Darwinians and Creationists is impossible to resolve. Darwinians and Creationists both have a system of beliefs that is founded on a version of faith. Darwinians have faith in the fossil record and scientific methods; the Creationists have faith in The Bible and the reality of a spiritual dimension to human affairs. Some would argue that faith, by definition, posits the existence of a reality other than the reality of the everyday world, but being faithful to a religious faith is different from being faithful to a spouse.

- In his desire to understand the principles of Greek tragedy, Nietzsche questioned the fundamental psychology of the Greeks. He pointed to the Greek love of beauty and wondered why, at the same time, they were attracted by ugliness and pain, which are the springs of tragedy. But he tended simply to ask questions, asking if the attraction of beauty was born of pain, admiring the Greeks' *joie de vivre* but at the same time asking if they were just melancholy by nature. Greek plays and poems were certainly characterized by fear, destruction and death but, at the same time, daily life in Greece seemed to be characterized by beauty and pleasure.

Chapter 7

Style and convention

As we keep insisting, you need to be aware of and consistent in your application of formal academic conventions. It would, though, be wrong to see them simply as restrictions on your natural imaginative impulses. They're not there to inhibit you, but to help you articulate your argument in a clear, recognizable form. It's therefore worth looking at some of the main aspects of these conventions to see how you can use them to your advantage and raise the standard of your work.

Nouns or verbs?

If we tried to cover all the possible combinations of 'weak' and 'strong' nouns and verbs in order to establish the 'ideal' structure for an effective sentence, you'd be swamped with examples and, rather than achieve the clarity we're seeking, we'd convey only confusion. It's a problem for all books and websites that give advice on writing and, sometimes, some of them carry misleading ideas about how language works. They identify 'weak' and 'strong' verbs and nouns, claim that the effectiveness of sentences depends more on nouns than verbs or vice versa, and propose guidelines that inhibit rather than release their readers' potential. If you followed advice, for example, which suggested that it was better to avoid 'weak' verbs, such as 'to be', you'd have to reject the powerful sentence 'God is love'.[1] And you might find it difficult to draw conclusions about the relative importance of nouns and verbs from the famous opening sentence of *Moby Dick*, 'Call me Ishmael'. Meaning

---

1 In fairness, it should be noted that this piece of advice is usually intended to eliminate unnecessarily extended constructions, such as 'The aim of this study is to . . .' instead of 'This study aims to . . .'.

and persuasion depend not just on individual words but on how they're combined.

The balance you establish between strong and weak elements, nouns and verbs, depends entirely on what you're trying to achieve. There are general observations we can make about the different effects created by using active or passive constructions, formal or informal expressions but, in the end, the choice is yours. All we can do is point out, again as generalizations, some of the more commonly accepted opinions about the effects of different preferences. Take, for example, the following sentences:

> Global warming is a threat to every living creature.
>
> Global warming threatens every living creature.

They say the same thing and yet there's a difference. Those who favour nouns would say that the first is 'stronger', while fans of verbs would prefer the second. It's true that the verb 'threatens' is more direct, more dramatic but, by emphasizing the action, it shrinks the meaning a little. The first sentence, on the other hand, presents us with a wider context and focuses more on the idea of threat and the implications of the action. We're not indicating any preference for one or the other; our intention is simply to show that opting for a verb construction or a noun construction does affect the way a reader may respond.

The sentences are examples of something called nominalization. That simply means the process of turning verbs and adjectives into nouns. Broadly speaking, it amounts to changing actions into concepts. Look at these pairings:

> We observed . . .
> Observations were made . . .
>
> Their weight increased.
> There was an increase in weight.
>
> The regulations must be implemented.
> There must be an implementation of the regulations.
>
> We will consider . . .
> Consideration will be given to . . .
>
> Researchers compared results.
> Comparisons were made of the results.

In each case, the second sentence is nominalized. Nouns are being made to do the work and that has the effect of making the writing sound more abstract, more formal, perhaps even 'more academic'. But it could also be said that such sentences sound less direct, less specific than those in which the meaning is conveyed more through verbs. Both versions are grammatically correct; neither is 'wrong' but the different stylistic choices do affect meaning.

One criticism of nominalization is that it seems to need more words to make its point.[2] In all the above examples, the nominalized version is indeed longer, but you must decide what impression you want to leave with the reader. A preference for verbs will tend to produce a direct, journalistic style, as in:

> Researchers found that, when companies sponsored local residents to renovate the neighbourhood, crime in the area decreased and the heavy police presence could be reduced.

Nominalization creates a less directly descriptive effect and shifts the focus away from the actions and onto the ideas behind them:

> Researchers found that renovation of the neighbourhood as a result of company sponsorship of local residents led to a decrease in crime in the area and a reduction in the scale of the police presence.

Longer extracts make it easier to appreciate how nominalization tends to convey an impression of wider concepts rather than specific, limited activities. Interestingly, though, in the following examples, the nominalized version has fewer words:

> Eating patterns were noticeably changed by eliminating direct nutrients, removing the primary stimulus and measuring by how much this reduced the amount the group members weighed. After that, by distributing supplements to some selected subjects and observing the ways in which they interacted with those carrying out the research, it was easier to evaluate how susceptible they were to secondary stimuli.

---

2 We're not suggesting by this that long sentences are 'bad'. Sometimes they need to convey a lot of connected information. We gave examples of the effect of long and short sentences in the previous chapter pp. 89–90.

The elimination of direct nutrients, the removal of the primary stimulus and the measurement of the resultant weight loss in group members caused noticeable changes in eating patterns. The subsequent distribution of supplements to a selection of subjects and observation of their interactions with the researchers facilitated an evaluation of their susceptibility to secondary stimuli.

So, nouns aren't 'better' than verbs or vice versa; it's a question of balancing the advantages of abstract and formal, direct and dramatic effects, wordiness and clarity. You don't have to choose between them, but it does help to be aware of their differences and sensitive to the stylistic nuances they offer you.

Abstract or concrete?

The relative value of using 'abstract' or 'concrete' words is the subject of a similar debate. Passion, philosophy, engineering, happiness, belief are all examples of abstract nouns; they identify ideas, concepts, principles – anything, in fact that's intangible. They have no physical shape or substance, and can't easily be defined. France, Tom, table, elephant, rain are concrete nouns; names of material objects, places and people. The obvious observation to make is that abstractions, being harder to pin down, seem more suited to speculative writing or conceptual arguments, while concrete nouns deal in facts. This, though, is a dangerous generalization. Once again, be aware of the different tone that they bring to your writing, but remember that there are no rules to say that you should use one rather than the other. Choose the words that will create the response you're looking for in your reader.

Formal or informal?

There is much variety in academic writing. It ranges from descriptions of factual scientific processes and experiments to analyses and evaluations of literary creativity. In most instances, however, the need is to present a well-argued case, supporting your reasoning with evidence and this, in turn, suggests that your preferred strategy should be to use formal rather than informal words or expressions. For example, instead of remarking that the findings of a political survey are 'astonishing' or 'mind-boggling', it would be safer to say that they're 'significant'; instead of writing a study that 'looks at' cognitive behavioural therapies, it would be better for it to 'consider' or 'examine' them.

'Looks at' is an example of a type of expression that's more commonly found in speech than in writing (unless the writing is aiming deliberately at achieving an informal effect). It's a phrasal verb, which means a verb to which one or more prepositions (or particles) are added to convey a specific meaning. The examples with which we began the book – run up, run across, run out of, run-down – show how the words that are added change the meaning completely, none of them having anything to do with actual running.[3] They're perfectly correct expressions and, indeed, they show the flexibility of the language, but they do tend to be conversational so, for the most part, if you come across examples in your first draft, it would probably be wise to replace them with a single verb.[4]

DIY

Phrasal verbs

The problem is that we use many expressions that, when we're speaking, are legitimate and appropriate, but which, if written, wouldn't work in the same way. They're called colloquialisms and you should try to avoid using them, especially in academic writing. Some of them are obvious. If you wrote, for example, that Shakespeare's sonnet sequence was 'a load of rubbish', you shouldn't expect much sympathy from your marker. Others, though, are less obvious and they creep into sentences and betray a bias that undermines rational argument. A historian who writes about the 'brutal' executions ordered by a particular regime or the 'unfortunate' victims of a political coup is revealing a lack of objectivity. Even apparently harmless words such as 'obviously' betray the fact that you may already have made your mind up about something. Words and expressions such as these are called value judgements. They show that you're not just describing or analysing what happened, you're judging it. That may be legitimate when you come to write a conclusion based on your findings but it shouldn't be evident in the analysis itself.

Value judgements reveal your personal opinion and are, therefore, subjective. In general terms, academic work requires you to observe, analyze and comment on issues in an objective, dispassionate and professional way, using formal rather than informal language and structures. Good academic writing is impersonal; it uses neutral language and usually tries to avoid relying on 'I', 'you', 'we', 'my', 'your' and

---

3 See introduction, p. 1.
4 For example, if we were using a more formal style in this paragraph, we would replace 'none of them having anything to do with actual running' with 'none of them involving actual running' and 'if you come across examples' with 'if you discover examples'.

'our' in its discussions of events, circumstances, ideas or actions.[5]
It presents its evidence, unclouded by preconceptions, and
balances arguments before expressing an opinion about where
they have led or might lead.

Having said that, we're encouraged by the fact that some
departments and institutions are beginning to acknowledge that
a rigid adherence to this convention can lead to a feeling of
lifelessness in the writing, a dullness that derives from an over-use of
passive and impersonal constructions, and the wordiness that's often
associated with them. Consequently, there are signs that some are willing
to accept the use of personal pronouns to allow you to express yourself
more simply, more directly and, perhaps, in a more lively and committed
way. That doesn't mean that you can get away with guesswork and
suppositions; your work still has to present the findings on which
you're basing your opinions, but you're not always obliged to hide
behind expressions such as 'It is evident that . . .', or 'This study
demonstrates that . . .'. It's a tendency that's welcomed by the advocates
of plain English but, before you start sprinkling your writing with 'I'
and 'my', check with your department or tutor to find out whether it's
acceptable.

Passive or active?

Personal pronouns are an important part of the active/passive debate.
For those of you who may be unsure about the difference, here are
two examples:

> University students often buy second-hand books. (ACTIVE)
>
> Second-hand books are often bought by university students.
>   (PASSIVE)

> We deprived the plants of water for six days. (ACTIVE)
>
> The plants were deprived of water for six days. (PASSIVE)

The active pattern is:

- actor/action/thing acted upon;
- students/buy/books;
- we/deprived/plants.

---

5 See the DIY task in Ch. 1 pp. 22–3.

The passive pattern is:

- thing acted upon/action/actor;
- books/are bought/by students;
- plants/were deprived/(by us).[6]

To generalize, the passive voice focuses attention on what's being done rather than on who or what is doing it. But it usually needs more words than the active voice and is often less easy to understand. 'Researchers conducted the experiment' is a more 'friendly' sentence than 'The experiment was conducted by researchers'. But, as ever, it's not that simple. If we expand it, we get:

> The researchers conducted the experiment to establish the reactions of subjects to negative stimuli.

> The experiment was conducted by researchers to establish the reactions of subjects to negative stimuli.

In this case, the passive form is more appropriate, perhaps even 'better' because the important information that's being conveyed is the nature and intention of the experiment. In the active version, 'The researchers' is prominent, but in the second, the passive construction focuses more directly on the experiment and, indeed, the words 'by researchers' could be omitted with affecting the meaning.

So, as we said, an active construction puts more emphasis on the person(s) performing the action, while a passive construction depersonalizes the action and tends to make the sentence seem more factual. The active is usually clearer, less confusing and uses fewer words but the passive has a more objective feel. In the end, though, the differences are more subtle than that and you'll need to develop your sensitivity to how they work. Here's another active/passive formulation. Read it and think about where the emphasis lies:

> Cognitive behavioural therapies have replaced Freudian treatments.

> Freudian treatments have been replaced by cognitive behavioural therapies.

---

6 Note that passive sentences don't always include the actor. Their focus is on the action.

The first – the active form – tends to suggest that cognitive behavioural therapies are more important than Freudian treatments. The second – the passive form – maintains a balance between them, giving them equal value. The same observation applies to the following examples:

> Our beliefs and perceptions shape the way we view the world.
>
> The way we view the world is shaped by our beliefs and perceptions.

We've quoted these to show that there's no rule about preferring one to the other. Each tips the meaning, if only slightly, in a particular direction. So use both, choose constructions that feel more comfortable for you and that help your reader to grasp your ideas.

Gender neutral language

In recent years, we've been encouraged to use language more sensitively when we're referring to individuals or groups of people. In our introduction we mentioned that we'd be using the pronouns 'he', 'she', 'his' and 'hers' in a random way and we explained why we'd chosen to do so. Gender stereotyping tends to slot individuals – male and female – into roles that can imply superiority, inferiority or some other inappropriate and unfounded relationship.

Language must be inclusive rather than exclusive but the need to maintain equality between the sexes can create serious problems for writers. Not simply by testing their political correctness, but by forcing them to create ugly sentences which are so unwieldy that their construction actually gets in the way of their meaning. Let's try a relatively simple example:

> A student needs to discipline himself or herself and ration his or her time so that he or she can be sure that his or her work does not suffer unduly because his or her leisure activities take precedence over his or her studies.[7]

---

7 There's a case for suggesting that this horrible sentence, even though it's trying desperately to stay 'fair', is still favouring the male because, each time there's a male-female alternative, the male version comes first and, therefore, is implicitly given precedence.

No-one would let such a sentence stand, but we're still left with the need to be inclusive. One way is to try to avoid gender-specific language but, sometimes, that obviously can't be done. Another is to use plural forms wherever possible. That would have solved all the problems in our example, which would become:

> Students need to discipline themselves and ration their time so that they can be sure that their work does not suffer unduly because their leisure activities take precedence over their studies.

Another technique that's used seems to provide a solution, as in the sentence: 'On arrival, each immigrant was expected to declare their country of origin'. The problem here, though, is that this is grammatically incorrect; 'each immigrant' is singular, 'their' is plural. Language is, of course, evolving all the time and some 'incorrect' usages are accepted as they're encountered more frequently but, with academic writing, it's safer not to take the chance of losing marks for 'bad' grammar.

The problems associated with gender-specific language have had lots of publicity over the years, but people have gradually come to accept the need to avoid using it. While still derided by some, the awareness of a need for politically correct language is now widespread. Age, disability, height, race, colour are all sensitive areas and, in your writing, you should make sure that you use inclusive rather than exclusive expressions. Thoughtless writing can be hurtful as well as offensive.

Abbreviations and acronyms

Many students get into the habit of using abbreviations when they take down notes from lectures or books, or just jotting down ideas. 'Information' becomes 'info', 'Shakespeare' becomes 'Sh' or 'Shak', 'Statistical analysis' becomes 'Stat an' and people create their own versions of words and expressions that they find occur frequently in their jottings. It makes sense because it saves time and space, but make sure that, when you're writing an assignment which is going to be marked, you write words and expressions out in full.

There are, however, occasions when abbreviations are not only permitted but helpful. In academic work, for example, you'll frequently have to use terminology that consists of relatively long words; they're part of the specialized vocabulary specific to the various disciplines. When they recur frequently, their repetition can be intrusive. The reader can't help noticing them and his attention is consequently drawn away from the overall argument you're presenting. Abbreviation helps you to deal with the problem. Each discipline has its own range of abbreviations and you'll often find lists of them in the glossary of a textbook. The most common ones are also listed in subject-specific dictionaries.

> **QR**
> Abbreviations for academic purposes

The first time one of these terms occurs in your text, write it out in full, with the abbreviation in brackets immediately after it. From that point on, having told (or reminded) your reader of what it stands for, you can just use the abbreviation. For example: 'Ethylene diamine tetra-acetic acid (EDTA) was introduced into the container. EDTA is necessary because . . .'[8]

Some standard abbreviations, such as *e.g.* and *i.e.* are so common that we often treat them as if they were words themselves. They stand for the Latin expressions, *exempli gratia* and *id est,* and there are many other Latin words that are abbreviated and have specific academic applications, such as *ibid.* and *cf.* Rather than list them here, we've identified them and explained how they're used in the Quick Reference section of the book. Before we leave this point, though, you should note that *e.g.* and *i.e.* are acceptable in science and engineering texts but, unless they're in diagrams or tables, you shouldn't use them for assignments in the Arts, Humanities and Social Sciences.

Acronyms are a different type of abbreviation. They bring the initial letters of a group of words together to make a word that's much shorter and easier to pronounce. Radar is an example we've already quoted, NATO is another. The trap to avoid when using such expressions is one of repetition. NATO, of course, stands for the North Atlantic Treaty Organization, so make sure you don't write about 'the NATO organization'.

Italics

You'll notice that we've used italics at several points in the book, most recently in the penultimate paragraph of the previous section. There are several conventions about when they should be used. Frequently in

---

8 Of course, there are some abbreviations which have become 'words' in their own right and don't need to be identified. Everyone has heard of radar, but not many know (or need to know) that it stands for **ra**dio **de**tection **an**d **r**anging. The same is true of DNA – deoxyribonucleic acid.

academic texts *e.g.* and *i.e.* are italicized since, in common with the other examples above, they are used as non-English expressions. Other examples are:

- The diplomatic community was stunned when the ambassador was declared *persona non grata*.
- The impact of *glasnost* was felt throughout the civilized world.
- As far as the observers were concerned, the capitulation was a *fait accompli*.
- The plant used in this investigation was *Phaseolus vulgaris*.

This last example also illustrates the fact that, in botany, zoology and other branches of science, terms relating to species are always printed in italics.

Some writers use italics to emphasize words, phrases, or even entire sentences, but it's a technique that's best avoided or, at least, used sparingly.

Footnotes and endnotes

As their names suggest, footnotes are placed at the foot of the page that contains the text to which they relate, while endnotes occur at the end of the chapter or book. The convention is to insert small superscript numbers in the text at the relevant point and write the note in a smaller font size beside the corresponding number at the foot of the page or end of the book/chapter. But when do you use them?

The answer to that may vary according to your particular discipline and you should find out your department's policy before you start writing.[9] In general terms, though, they have two main functions:

- In some referencing systems they carry your bibliographical references.
- They add further information that is relevant to the text but not essential to an understanding of the point you're making.

Some people say that, if the information they contain isn't essential to your argument, it needn't be included, but there are times when an extra piece of information may reinforce a line of reasoning, or perhaps

---

9 It may be in the course handbook.

introduce a note of caution. The important point is that, if the information is put into a little parcel that is separate from the text, it doesn't interfere with your overall flow.

If you do decide to use footnotes or endnotes, or if your department requires you to do so, be consistent in how you format and write them.

Appendices

In a way, appendices are very long endnotes (although no academic would give us a good mark for saying such a thing). Normally, they're listed as Appendix A, B, C or 1, 2, 3 and their pages are numbered with lower case Roman numerals – i, ii, iii.

An appendix is a chapter-like section at the end of a piece of academic writing, such as a project, report, dissertation or thesis, which carries information closely related to what's written in the main body of the work. Usually, it consists of extra material that may develop specific issues or add to the reader's understanding of a particular point or series of points. Frequently, it's very detailed and, if you left it in with the main text, it might clog it up and slow the development of your argument.

From all of the above, and from the comments we made in the previous chapter, it should be obvious that style is a flexible concept. If we could simply offer you some 'rules' to follow, we would, but academic writing, for all that it seems to be instantly identifiable, is as textured and nuanced as any other type of writing that seeks to persuade the reader. Its conclusions should be based on objective evidence, it should avoid loose constructions and value judgements, and it should make the reader clearly aware of your meaning. By learning to channel your thoughts to achieve these ends, you'll not only become more proficient at using language, you'll also be helping yourself to think more clearly.

DIY TASK I

Nominalization

Use nominalization on the following passages and, when you've completed each, compare the two versions to test the differences in tone and effect. You may have to add words or change things to accommodate them:

- The fact that couples were encouraged by the government to limit their families to two children led everyone to expect that, within a generation, they would solve the problem of there being too many citizens. However, it was difficult to implement the scheme. Those who were administering it complained that its terms of reference were too wide and that they found it very difficult to control its budgets.

- As a result of the country being invaded, its army fragmented and sections of the militia helped to form breakaway groups. These were responsible for continuing to fight after peace had been negotiated. It was only when they were dispersed that food could be distributed and the people could begin to enjoy being independent.

- Hugo remained convinced that he was superior to all other writers, a belief which led him to embrace spiritualist practices in his later years. His tireless efforts at being perfect were ultimately rejected and ridiculed by those who witnessed them.

- The subjects were willing to wait for their results to be analysed.

Now try reversing the techniques to reword these nominalizations as verbs. Once again, note the differences between the two versions:

- Observations of mass hysteria in the congregations at the rallies led to the researchers' conclusion that hypnosis was a contributory factor to the elevation and enrichment of the cult and that judicial action would be necessary to ensure its eradication.

- A simple statement conveys the basic tenet of existentialism – existence precedes essence.

- There was a convincing demonstration by worshippers in the second group that a strongly held conviction led to the transformation of fragility into strength.

DIY TASK 2

Phrasal verbs

Replace the phrasal verbs in the following paragraph with single verbs or nouns:

• The team leader brought together the questionnaires and put them in order to make it easier for her to think about the various ways they could be used to put across the department's current attitude towards the issue. She came across a few inconsistencies but realized that they would have to put up with some discrepancies if they wanted to find out the underlying truth. The team broke up into smaller units to look into different aspects of the findings and talk about how they compared with wider political thinking. Respondents who had refused to look more closely at the alternatives being offered had thrown out many valuable options, many forcefully putting across the fact that they looked the same as the proposals they had already got rid of. They preferred to cut out the more expensive solutions, try out everything in the middle range and make their minds up when they had been told about how much money was going to be made available.

DIY TASK 3

Value judgements

Check these sentences to identify any words or expressions that betray bias on the part of the writer and rewrite them as objective contributions to an argument:

- Naturally enough, the statistics produced by the Department of Health confirm the bias evident in those which have been published with such blatant self-satisfaction by the Treasury.

- Leading experts in the field of paediatric bioethics continue to argue that conducting research on children is the only way to combat diseases such as cystic fibrosis. This questionable research consists of arbitrary procedures that submit healthy children to painful and dangerous treatments. The unfortunate child is often too young to be able to refuse these intrusive experiments and the risks are usually brushed aside by researchers more concerned with publishing their results than with the damage they are causing.

- Labour laws have been amended to accommodate the need to acknowledge the growing importance of the disadvantaged immigrant community. Despite being subjected to treatment that is frankly inhuman, illegal immigrants are courageous enough to seek to establish themselves in the UK. In their desperation, they are prepared to do the most degrading jobs. They are not unionized, they have no leverage when it comes to negotiating pay and conditions and, if they are unfortunate enough to sustain an injury in the course of their work, they have no right to any compensation.

Chapter 8

Making it better

A professional approach

At the start, we suggested breaking down the process of writing an assignment into various phases. So far, we've looked at understanding the question, collecting then organizing the material, and writing. That just leaves editing and proofreading.

Quite often, the first reaction as you finish writing is one of relief. You're glad it's over and all you want to do is hand it in and relax until the next assignment's set. It's an understandable impulse, but one that could have negative results. All writers, even the best ones, make mistakes and, in academic writing, that means losing marks. It also suggests a carelessness in the way you're approaching your studies and a lack of professionalism. You've worked hard on gathering, organizing and transcribing the material, so it makes sense to check it thoroughly before you submit it. You want to present the person who's marking it with the best possible example of the way you work.

Part of the problem is that word-processed copy, when it's printed out, looks fine and so gives the impression that it's a professional job. But that would also be the case if the document consisted of words and expressions chosen randomly from phone books or clothing catalogues. Don't be fooled by the superficial appearance of the printed page. Yes, it has to be neat, but that's just the packaging. Layout, font size, paragraph markers and the like are all important in that they help the reader, but it's the argument and the details of how it's presented that earn the marks.

Before you start, take a break – establish a distance between you-the-writer and you-the-editor. In Chapter 5 we pointed out that such a separation of roles is artificial but it does help you to pace yourself and make sure you cover all the bases. So, if you've planned your time carefully, you should now be able to go away and do something un-connected with the assignment, try to forget about it and clear your mind of all the thoughts and ideas that have been so central to your thinking as you've been working on it.

When you do start the editing, do it with the same care you've applied to all the preceding phases. It's not enough just to use your word-processing programme to do a spell check or grammar check; editing calls for concentration, attention to detail and judgements relating to style and content that are beyond any automated process. You'll be checking whether your interpretation of the question is accurate and whether you truly have responded to it in the way the wording asked you to. You'll be assessing it for relevance, objectivity, clarity and overall sense. You'll be asking whether sentences make sense (and even whether they actually are sentences). It's a demanding task but, if you're system-atic about it, you can eliminate the weaknesses that could lose you marks.

Reading aloud

When reading, we tend to see what we want or expect to see rather what is on the page. For example, we deliberately left the word 'than' out of the preceding sentence. Some of you will have noticed it, others may not have. All the time, our minds are moving ahead, making sense of things, filling the gaps. When we see a familiar sequence of words, we anticipate that they'll all be there and so we skim to the next sequence. This tendency is even more marked when we're reading a text that we've written ourselves. We read what we meant to say rather than what we said.

That's why, when editing, it's helpful to use some artificial means to change the way you read. You could put a ruler or a piece of paper under each line as you read it to stop your eyes jumping ahead; you could trace the words with your finger; you could read paragraphs out of sequence (which would help you to spot mistakes, omissions and awkward expressions but not to gauge the flow of your argument). You could even start from the last page and work your way back to the first. They're all ways of forcing you to approach the writing in a different way. Best of all – and a technique which we'd suggest is essential – is to read the text aloud, making sure that you're being both reader and listener.

It may feel strange or silly to be sitting in a room on your own pretending to be a newsreader, but it's an excellent way of approaching your work from a different angle. Don't rush the reading; keep it slow so that it would make sense to anyone listening and make sure you concentrate hard on hearing and understanding what you're saying. It's important to keep that focus, so we'd recommend that you don't try to deal with more than two or three pages at a time. Read them, make any changes that are needed, then take a break before coming back to the next few pages.

It will help you in several ways. On the page, it isn't always easy to spot repetitious use of particular words or phrases but, when you hear them, they become obvious. The same is true of sentences that are too long or too short, or sentences that aren't sentences at all. The following is a fairly common mistake:

> As a consequence of gathering data from both pre-qualified medical orderlies and those who were still following a course of studies. Profiles were available for all candidates in the main hospitals in the catchment area.

This should, of course, be a single sentence. As it stands, the first part – up to the first full stop – makes no sense on its own.

Reading aloud is particularly helpful in indicating where you need (and don't need) punctuation marks. If you read properly, grouping and stressing the words to convey their sense, you'll find that you have to pause at particular points. If you do so and you find that there's no punctuation mark there, there probably should be. Equally, if you read the above example and stopped at 'studies' because of the full stop, you'd realize that the sentences should be linked and you'd replace the stop with a comma.

DIY

Punctuation

Remember, you wrote your assignment for a reader; now you're being that reader. If it's not easy to read, it needs attention. Help the reader by inserting 'signposts', by creating clear links between paragraphs and sentences, or pointing out when the meaning is moving in a different direction. When you're reading, if a sentence feels strange – even if it's only a vague feeling – stop, isolate it from the rest of the text and check it thoroughly to establish where the problem is and rectify it.

One final point about the value of reading aloud concerns rhythm. We mentioned the metronome effect in Chapter 6; it occurs when sentences are all of a similar length, especially if they're short. As you read, you should feel that there's variation in tone and pitch, but that the meaning runs on smoothly. On the other hand, if it's being chopped into small, regular bunches, you won't be able to maintain the flow because you have to keep stopping. As soon as you realize that this is happening, stop and try to vary the length of the sentences so that you restore a more fluid delivery.

Common mistakes

Overall, you're checking for grammar, spelling, style and how the argument flows. You're looking for consistency in the way you use capitals, italics, underlinings and quotation marks. You should be aware, too, of the sort of mistakes you yourself make most often and search for them specifically.

There are also some types of error that seem to occur with greater frequency than others. They're mistakes that we all make and, while there are too many to list, it's useful to identify the most common ones.

Subject/verb agreement

It's unlikely that you'd make the mistake of writing 'the students is tired' or 'the student are tired', but failing to follow a singular subject with the singular form of the verb, or a plural with a plural, is surprisingly common. Sometimes it occurs because there are other words, phrases or clauses between them and they're so far separated that it's difficult to be sure of what the subject is. For example:

> The local representative, uncertain as to the extent of her powers and dependent on the support of groups and individuals spread throughout all the counties of the south west, were ready to vote for constitutional change.

DIY

Subject/verb
agreement

Here, the subject is 'the local representative' and the verb is 'were' and, again, you wouldn't write 'The local representative were ready'.

It also happens when the subject consists of more than one element, as in 'the writing of complex essays are difficult'. The subject here is 'writing', so it needs a singular verb.

There are, of course, some subjects that can be treated as both singular and plural. It's equally legitimate, for example, to write 'the government was prepared to compromise' and 'the government were prepared to compromise'. The only problem that might then arise is one of consistency. It's all too easy to make the government both singular and plural in the same sentence, as in 'The government is prepared to compromise and they have already published an amended version of the bill'.

In some instances, opting for singular rather than plural actually changes the meaning. 'The group was small' means that there were very few people in it, but 'The group were small' refers to the height of its members.

Sequence of tenses

The tense of a verb usually depends on its context and few would make a mistake such as: 'After they had gathered the data, they measure its relevance'. But, where the sequence of events isn't so clear, it's quite easy to lose track of tenses, especially when you're referring to the findings of others. The following example is rather long, but it shows how a careless writer can move back and forth between present and past:

> In their paper, the researchers demonstrate that, although the terms 'force' and 'interaction' are often seen as interchangeable concepts, their meanings are clearly distinct from one another. Their experiments proved that every force, attractive or repulsive, from friction to electromagnetism, from gravitational attraction to nuclear decay, was the result of fundamental particle interactions. A force could therefore be defined as something which acted on a particle because of the presence of other particles, whereas an interaction can encompass every force acting on it, including those of decay and annihilation.

The need, as we've pointed out in connection with many other aspects of writing, is for consistency. Decide which tense best suits your argument and then stick to it.

Pronouns and prepositions

'The letter was sent from I to you' is clearly wrong, and yet people still manage not to notice that 'I told them it was from you and I' is the same mistake. 'This is between you and I' is as bad grammatically as 'Me have to write an essay'.

When a pronoun is the subject of a verb, it's 'I', 'he', 'she', 'we' or 'they'. When it's the object, it's 'me', 'him', 'her', 'us' or 'them'. ('It' and 'you' don't change.) That applies not only when it's a direct object, as in 'They believed her', but also when it's an indirect object; in other words, when it has a preposition, as in 'They gave it to her' and 'There was little to choose between him and me'.

As well as making sure that you choose the right case for the pronoun, which is what we've just been doing, it's important to check that you've chosen the right pronoun for the context. 'If a student has an important exam to sit, they should get plenty of rest' is, of course, wrong; 'they' should be 'he' or 'she'. A pronoun always refers to something; it may be a noun, as in the previous example, but it may be a much wider construction. In the following extract, 'this' refers to a complex of ideas:

> Louis XVI and Marie Antoinette preferred the artificiality of life at Versailles to the squalor surrounding them at the Louvre. This alienated peasant and bourgeois alike.

If you don't make sure that it's easy for the reader to see what your pronouns are referring to, you risk loss of meaning or ambiguity. Let's take some examples:

- 'The President refused to accept the ultimatum of the Prime Minister. It was obvious that he was exceeding his authority.'
  Who was? The President or the Prime Minister?

- 'The article questioned the evidence which the research claimed to have disclosed. It was biased.'
  What was? The article? The evidence? The research?

- 'The powers of monarchs are tacitly endorsed by the citizens and subjects of their states while those of elected governments sometimes seem precarious. They demonstrate the fallibility of constitutional rigidity.'
  To what does 'they' refer? There are several possibilities: powers, monarchs, citizens and subjects, states, those, governments. Some of these are clearly more likely candidates than others, but the ambiguities cloud the meaning.

Just as choosing the right pronoun depends upon context, so, too, does choosing the right preposition. To give just one example, things are 'different from' other things, not 'different to' or 'different than'.

Comparisons

Expressions that include words such as 'different' usually imply some sort of comparison, and it's important to make sure that you compare like with like. In the sentence 'The findings of the social work committee provided a more reliable indicator than the chairman', a comparison is being made between findings and a person. The correct version would read 'The findings of the social work committee provided a more reliable indicator than those of the chairman'.

DIY

Comparisons

It's very easy to make such errors, especially in longer constructions. Whenever you have two or more sets of words, phrases or clauses being compared or linked in some other relationship, make sure that you use the same grammatical construction for each. In the following sentence, for example, the subject is 'responsible for' three things, but two of them are expressed as nouns and the third as a verb:

> Surgical intervention was responsible for the perceived variations in survival rates, demographic stability and increasing the life span of older residents.

A 'correct' version of the final element would be '. . . the increase in the life span . . .'.

Hanging participle

An oft-quoted example of a hanging participle is 'Walking down the High Street, there's a tree on the left hand side'. It's obviously wrong because it implies that the tree is doing the walking. Participles vary greatly and can be formed in different ways. 'Following' is a participle, so is 'followed'. Our intention here, though, isn't to offer a grammar lesson on them but to point out a common misuse.

An example of 'correct' usage is 'When applying for funding, the head of the project was aware of its probable costs'. The participle 'applying' relates to the subject of what follows – 'the head of the project'. If we'd written 'When applying for funding, the project was probably going to be expensive', that would suggest that it was the project that was doing the applying. So, when you use constructions involving participles, make sure that they don't 'hang' on their own, but that they relate to the appropriate element in the main clause.

Too many nouns

Say you lived in Aberdeen and you were interested in history appreciation. If that was the case, you might want to join the Aberdeen History Appreciation Society and perhaps go to an Aberdeen History Appreciation Society Lecture, in which case, you'd want to consult the Aberdeen History Appreciation Society Lecture Programme and so you'd contact the Aberdeen History Appreciation Society Lecture Programme Organizer. The final seven words of that sentence make sense, but they create an awkward, ugly impression and they obviously need some other types of words (verbs, prepositions) to make them easier to read and understand. 'The person who organizes the lecture programme for the History Appreciation Society in Aberdeen' is still long-winded but it's much better balanced, and therefore more comprehensible, than the phrase it's replacing.

Too many words

Bafflingly, airport announcers nearly always broadcast a 'last and final call for passengers travelling to' somewhere or other on flight something or other. Recently, this has grown into a 'last and very final call'. In a way, 'first and final' would make more sense – at least it would mean that there was only going to be one call, but 'last' and 'final' mean the same thing. It's an example of tautology, *i.e.* saying the same thing twice in different words.

When we're talking, we often use more words than we need to. There are various reasons for this. Few of us think in clearly delineated paragraphs and we're often groping for appropriate words and expressions; we use words and sounds to fill gaps. And we develop strange usages. One particularly baffling one is when people are relaying a conversation they've had. Very often, they say 'She turned round to me and said . . . and I turned round to her and said . . .'. If the words were taken literally they'd convey a picture of a chat between whirling dervishes. But the words mean nothing more than 'she said' and 'I said'.

When you write your assignment, your aim is clarity. Adding unnecessary words to emphasize or modify something often serves only to obscure it. 'What is clear is that the results are positive' means 'the results are positive'. 'There's absolutely no change whatsoever' means 'There's no change'. You don't join things 'together', you just join them. So beware of wordiness. The temptation to crowd your text to give it density, academic

DIY

Too many words

'respectability' or substance will have the opposite effect; the meaning will be buried under excess verbiage.

Numbers and amounts

Finally, there's the familiar confusion over when to use 'much' or 'many', 'less' or 'fewer'. The rule is simple, if you can count something (one exam, two lectures, frequent snow showers), you use 'many' and 'fewer'; if you can't count it (research, importance, food), you use 'much' and 'less'.

Ne plus ultra

Ne plus ultra was inscribed on the Pillars of Hercules in the straits of Gibraltar. Literally, it means 'not further beyond'. In other words, this is as far as you can go. Today, we use it to refer to something that is flawless and, if you've been thorough with your editing, that's what the piece of work you're about to hand in should be. It may contain flawed arguments or misunderstandings but, in terms of the way you've presented it, it's as clear, uncluttered and, stylistically and grammatically, as 'correct' as you can make it.

Your final checks can concentrate on general presentational features. Make sure, for example, that you've formatted it in the way that's approved by your department. Is it double spaced? Is the font size correct? Have you used footnotes or endnotes and numbered them properly? Are your bibliography and list of references complete and consistent? When you're satisfied that the answer in each case is 'yes', the job's done and you'll have made sure that, if you do lose any marks, it won't be through carelessness or a lack of professionalism. Step by step, you've reached the summit.

DIY TASK 1

Punctuation

We've removed all the punctuation (including apostrophes) from this passage. Use it to show how reading aloud will help you to see where the gaps occur and where you need to add the relevant punctuation marks:

- according to recent research the difficulties involved in educating children at home whichever part of the country they live in are exacerbated by the authorities failure to devote sufficient funds to effective support systems those parents whose efforts have in some cases delivered excellent results have had to devote often stretched resources to remedy the shortfall we never know where we are said one of the respondents to the most recent questionnaire its always the same the council registers our enquiries then ignores them and carries on with its own agenda there does however appear to be a relatively simple solution and administrators have identified three fast effective processes which parents can adopt online access by means of a password-protected account certification at the local education authority and direct bank transfers these suggestions have met with a degree of scepticism which some would say is the inevitable consequence of a systemic failure at every level.

DIY TASK 2

Subject/verb agreement

Check and correct the agreements between subjects and verbs in this short paragraph:

- The consequence of several depositions being made to the courts within a relatively short period are self-evident. Administrators, bound by their commitment to the wider judicial process and aware of their responsibility to a central committee, is laden with a barely tolerable burden. A flawed appeals process, a continuous preference for self-interested interpretations, and a failure to allow due time to complete the application procedure is leading to the progressive weakening of the law itself. Those charged with modernizing the system claim that the combination of greed, hypocrisy and 'ambulance chasers' are a recipe for chaos.

DIY TASK 3

Comparisons

Here are more badly written sentences for you to correct. This time, various expressions stating or implying comparisons need your attention:

- The results of the American experiments differed significantly from the Europeans. Decisions on reinvestment of profits were made by middle management rather than resource-dependent. In Europe, less attention was paid to quarterly statements and projections than to balancing the budget at the end of the financial year. Americans seem less concerned with long-term fluctuations than making short-term gains.

- The debate on the welfare of animals used in research involves not only scientists but also theologians, philosophers and legislation. These animals are, in a way, as much a part of the research team as the results it produces, and they therefore deserve the respect of those working with them. In the seventeenth century, the consciousness of animals was compared with humans and dismissed as being non-existent but, in the nineteenth century, society began to develop a greater sensitivity to suffering and it was suggested that human pain was on a par with animals. Finally, when Darwin placed humankind firmly in, rather than apart from, the animal kingdom, it was the stimulus for a move towards the first legislation designed to protect animals from the hitherto unlimited whims of the scientists and cruelty.

DIY TASK 4

Too many words

We've mentioned tautology. 'A vacuum is nothing but an empty void' is an example of the sort of nonsense it can produce. There are many – perhaps less obvious – examples in the following paragraph. You may need to use a dictionary to work out all of them but the object is to rewrite the paragraph in order to eliminate them all. When you've done so, you'll see again how useful and important it is to cut out excess. Writing is always better for being cut:

- The general consensus of opinion is that the complete elimination of greenhouse gas emissions is absolutely essential to the continued survival of our species. Martyn Gillespie, who is the chief protagonist of the carbon trading lobby, has proposed a temporary reprieve by adopting a policy which may possibly suggest that compromise is a viable option. His group is small in size but, at this moment in time, it is gaining in credibility. His opponents would do well to recognize its potential for growth and adapt their future plans in order to give advance warning of the complete monopoly Gillespie is beginning to construct. Nothing short of total unanimity will do. Researchers who care about the environment around them must spell out in detail the disastrous consequences that could arise if Gillespie were to prevail.

DIY TASK 5

Numbers and amounts

As usual, we've scattered mistakes through this paragraph for you to identify and correct:

- Competition is an essential part of progress. The more energy one directs towards attaining higher levels of competence, the greater the rewards. Psychologists claim that, since the 1990s, less people have expressed contentment with a static self-perception. The amount of middle-aged women following sustained fitness regimes has almost doubled and much of the current research projects are producing unexpected results. There is less obesity, less visits to GPs and less sweets and chocolates on the average shopping list. Indeed, there are even less lists. If further evidence confirms that much more changes are being made the need will be for a revaluation of the many parameters that measure perceptual norms.

Conclusion

Be true to yourself

As we said at the outset, our aims are to demystify the process of writing at university and to help you to liberate your potential. The idea isn't that you should adopt our suggestions and follow them slavishly as if they were a set of rules; we'd rather you used them to help you to develop your own way of working. Students aren't clones; what works for one may not work for another, so there's no single way of preparing for or writing an assignment.

Whichever technique you evolve, try to rationalize it into a sequence of minor tasks that combine to produce the completed assignment. Broadly speaking, those tasks will begin with research and move through writing to editing, so the activity has its own inherent logic that will affect the working method you choose. By recognizing that you're faced not with one huge task but with a series of smaller ones, you'll be better able to organize your time and have more confidence in your ability to produce a well-thought-out piece of work.

We've tried to highlight some of the traps into which students can fall. Remember the main ones:

- The best academic writing is clear. You'll use subject-specific terminology but don't be tempted to descend to jargon or to long words and tangled expressions that are meant to impress rather than communicate clearly.
- Write what the assignment's asking of you, not what you'd like it to be asking.
- You're writing to be read, so make sure the reader always knows where she is and how you're linking the various threads of your argument. If you write something that leaves the reader wondering

why it's there, you're creating a negative impression and probably losing marks.

- Take care to avoid value judgements. Your tone should be neutral and your claims should be substantiated by evidence.
- When you're writing, try not to do anything to interrupt the flow of your ideas. You can (and must) always iron out inconsistencies or linguistic problems at the editing stage.
- Never plagiarize.
- Don't rely on quotations to do the work for you. The reader's interested in your arguments, not those of other people, so don't drop them into your text without saying why you're using them and/or developing their point.
- When you're editing, read your work aloud, listen carefully to it and correct any sentences that sound awkward or in which the meaning isn't clear.
- Check your punctuation and the flow of your argument. Eliminate faulty spelling and grammar, intrusive repetitions and awkward stylistic constructions.
- Make sure that your list of references and your bibliography are correct and consistent. It shows that you're taking the work seriously and acting in a professional manner.
- When you're getting towards the end of an assignment, you'll want to hand it in and relax, but don't be fooled by a smart-looking printout. Word processors can make any written document look better than it is.

Try not to think of the writing as a self-contained activity whose sole purpose is to gain marks or credits. A university education should make us more aware of who, where and why we are. It should encourage us to question our assumptions. The process of finding the words and sequences to articulate our ideas does more than clarify our thinking, it actually generates the thoughts themselves. So be more aware of words, increase your vocabulary, acquire a wider referential range. Read books and articles but also good newspapers, with extended coverage of issues rather than just stories that serve up snippets and trivia and condense news into a patchwork of clichés. Reading is fundamental to writing.

In the Introduction, we suggested that there's more than one 'you' involved in this whole process. At that point, we were referring to you having to be a researcher, a writer and an editor. Then, in the first chapter, we noted how having to write down a thought commits you, forces you to turn it from an elusive, phantom thing into a 'fact'. When you put those two thoughts together, they create an interesting scenario. The different versions of 'you' are working together to generate, clarify and fix an intellectual 'reality' or 'truth'. Someone else will then examine, assess and grade that 'truth' and the grade will appear beside your name.

In other words, there's another 'you' – the one that's being marked. When you hand in the assignment, you've no control over how it'll be received; the 'you' on the page is the one that'll be judged. It's therefore very much in your interest to make sure that that particular 'you' is the real one, that what it's saying is an accurate encapsulation of your thinking on the topic in question. Taking care with your writing is a way of affirming who you are. So don't resort to gimmicks, parody or plagiarism; don't try to fool yourself or others. Have the confidence to be you.

Quick reference

Abbreviations for academic purposes

You need to understand how abbreviations are used in academic writing because, even though you may not need to use them yourself, you'll need to know what they mean when you come across them. Here are some examples of the more common ones.

In some referencing systems, abbreviations, often of Latin words, are used as a kind of 'shorthand code' to help you navigate through the reference list. The most commonly used are:

> *op. cit.* – *opere citato*: work already cited earlier in the reference list;
> *ibid.* – *ibidem* (in the same place): same details as the immediately previous citation;
> *cf.* – *confer*: compare;
> ed./edn: edition;
> ed./eds: editor/editors;
> p./pp.: page/pages.

In some disciplines, it's acceptable to use the following Latin abbreviations in text:

> *e.g.* (*exempli gratia*): for example;
> *i.e.* (*id est*): that is;
> *viz.* – *videlicet*: namely.

Note that, in many disciplines, the use of *e.g.*, *i.e.* and *viz.* in text is not accepted convention. In such instances, the full expressions 'for example', 'that is' and 'namely' should be used and should be followed by a comma if the first phrase in a sentence; or preceded and followed by commas if these expressions are positioned mid-sentence. However, if these expressions are being used to introduce a list of bullet points or a longer example, then they should be followed by a colon.

Alternative sources of information

Once you've identified the task you have to complete, it's worth considering all the sources of information at your disposal. We've noted some suggestions in this diagram. There'll be others that are specific to your discipline but here are some broad categories to get you started.

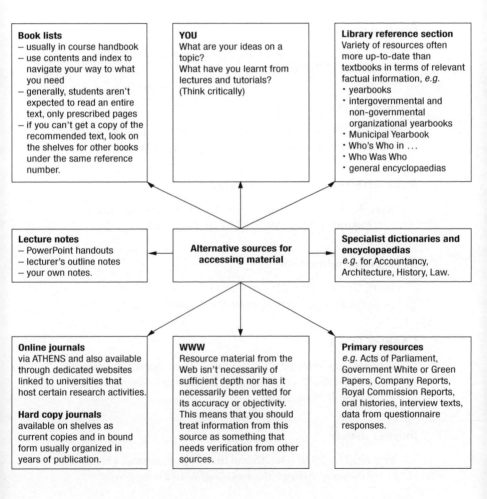

Book lists
– usually in course handbook
– use contents and index to navigate your way to what you need
– generally, students aren't expected to read an entire text, only prescribed pages
– if you can't get a copy of the recommended text, look on the shelves for other books under the same reference number.

YOU
What are your ideas on a topic?
What have you learnt from lectures and tutorials?
(Think critically)

Library reference section
Variety of resources often more up-to-date than textbooks in terms of relevant factual information, *e.g.*
• yearbooks
• intergovernmental and non-governmental organizational yearbooks
• Municipal Yearbook
• Who's Who in ...
• Who Was Who
• general encyclopaedias

Lecture notes
– PowerPoint handouts
– lecturer's outline notes
– your own notes.

Alternative sources for accessing material

Specialist dictionaries and encyclopaedias
e.g. for Accountancy, Architecture, History, Law.

Online journals
via ATHENS and also available through dedicated websites linked to universities that host certain research activities.

Hard copy journals
available on shelves as current copies and in bound form usually organized in years of publication.

WWW
Resource material from the Web isn't necessarily of sufficient depth nor has it necessarily been vetted for its accuracy or objectivity. This means that you should treat information from this source as something that needs verification from other sources.

Primary resources
e.g. Acts of Parliament, Government White or Green Papers, Company Reports, Royal Commission Reports, oral histories, interview texts, data from questionnaire responses.

Bibliographies and reference lists

For the purposes of this book, we've followed the Harvard method of referencing. It's used in a number of different disciplines, perhaps because it's relatively simple to follow and doesn't need double-entries in text. The format for this method is prescribed in BS5605:1990 but some of the punctuation conventions have been amended by publishing houses to suit their own particular house-style. This means that there may be some more modern variations of interpretation that differ slightly from the British Standard. The important thing is to make sure that whatever referencing system you use, you apply it with consistency.

Book with one author

Gordon, K., 2005. *The synthesis of C-glycosides.* Edinburgh: Pentland Publications.

Book with two authors

McKeith, G. and Millan, F.M., 2006. *Offshore wind farms: the alternative to wave power.* Orkney: Viking Press.

Book with three or more authors

Ross, F., Thain, M., and Baxter, A., 1999. *Food hygiene in hospital contexts.* Perth: Fair City Publishers.

Book under editorship

Scott, I., ed., 2006. *Mathematics for students of electronic engineering.* Northallerton: Dales Publishing.

Chapter in a book

Graham, F., 1994. Literacy in postmodern educational systems. In J. Stafford, ed., *Learning, language and literacy.* Luton: Magister Publications.

Journal article

Hunter, M., 2001. The African dream: post-colonial enterprise. *Journal of African Business Studies,* 4 (2), 39–45.

Frequently asked questions

What is the difference between a bibliography and a reference list?

A **bibliography** is a list of all books, journals and other resources, along with their publication details, that you've consulted in the process of producing a piece of written work.

A **reference list** comprises only those books, journals and other resources, along with their publication details, that you've referred to either directly by quotation or indirectly by summarizing ideas from those sources in your own work.

How should I lay out my bibliography/reference list?

In some interpretations of the Harvard method, the first line of every entry is indented by five character spaces. Other interpretations begin the first line of the entry on the left-hand margin and indent the subsequent lines by five character spaces.

How do I reference two resources published by the same author in the same year?

In this instance, the entries are given as the same year followed by lower case a, b, c and so on, for example, Smith (2006a), Smith (2006b).

How should I print the titles of books?

Titles of books should be printed in italics. In the Harvard method, for example, only the initial letter of the first word of the title should be capitalized. All other words with the exception of proper nouns should be in lower case.

What is secondary referencing and how do I include this in my text and in my references?

Ideally in your written work you cite only those texts that you've read yourself. But sometimes texts cited in other books you've read are out of print or not easy to get in the time you have available. If you want to cite these secondary references, you need to follow some simple conventions within the Harvard format.

Imagine, for example, that you've read a book by Jock Tamson published in 1996 entitled 'Highland Heritage' in which the writer referred to a statement about how Celtic crosses in Scottish churchyards provide a narrative of early Scottish history and that this is derived from a book written by Angus McKay published in 1983 under the title 'Celts and their history'. In this instance, this might be referred to in the text in the following way:

> McKay (1983 cited in Tamson, 1996) suggested that Celtic crosses found in many Scottish country churchyards provide a rich source of Scottish historical narrative.

or

> Tamson (1996) supports the view of McKay (1983) that the narrative of early Scottish history can be traced through Celtic crosses, many of which are found in Scottish country churchyards.

Following the Harvard method, in the bibliography/reference list, only the book you read, that is Tamson (1996), would be included.

I've been told to use a name/date system for my reference list. Is this the same as the Harvard method?

The Harvard method is often described as a name/date system. This means that the name of the author followed by the date of publication is given in the text and the following sequence is used in the reference at the single author level: (sur)name of author, initial, date of publication, title, place of publication and publisher.

We've mentioned three other more commonly used systems in this book. They might be defined in the following way:

- Chicago method: superscript numbers in the text immediately following the cited point.
- Modern Languages Association (MLA): name/page system in text.
- Vancouver method: numerical system with full-size numerals in brackets after the relevant point in the text.

If you need more information on any of these styles, your university library should be able to provide you with a reference to the relevant style guide.

British and American English

The familiar quip is that the USA and Great Britain are two nations divided by a single language. Elsewhere in the book we've referred to some differences between British and American English with regard to academic writing but the main points you need to be aware of are listed below.

Spelling differences:

- -our at the end of words and inside other words formed from them becomes, in American English -or
  - harbour, favour, favourite, behavioural (British)
  - harbor, favor, favorite, behavioral (American).

- -ise, -ising, -isation at the end of words become, in American English ize, izing, ization
  - customise, plagiarising, realisation (British)
  - customize, plagiarizing, realization (American).

- -re at the end of words and inside other words formed from them becomes, in American English -er
  - theatre, litre, centred (British)
  - theater, liter, centered (American).

- In British English, practise is the verb form, practice is the noun form. In American English, it's practice for both
  - Practice makes perfect, so she's practising her bunker shots. (British)
  - Practice makes perfect, so she's practicing her bunker shots. (American).

Note, too, how words ending in -el are spelled when -ed is added:

- Travelled, labelled, double-barrelled (British)
- Traveled, labeled, double-barreled (American).

Differences in punctuation:

- British English uses single and American English double quotation marks to indicate speech and quotations. For a quotation within a quotation, the reverse is, naturally, the case

   - 'Hamlet's answer "Words, words, words" emphasises the irony of his inaction.' (British)
   - "Hamlet's answer 'Words, words, words' emphasizes the irony of his inaction." (American)

When a sentence ends with a quotation mark, the British put the full stop outside the quotation mark, the Americans put it inside:

   - According to the authors of the report, 'a continued failure to respond to the current environmental policy will provoke extreme demographic change'. (British)
   - According to the authors of the report, "a continued failure to respond to the current environmental policy will provoke extreme demographic change." (American)

Difference between spoken and written language

Below are three examples that have been written on the topic of the extent to which people read newspapers:

Child writing

I don't read a newspaper very often but if I do I like the cartoons and the pictures and sometimes I like the music pages when there's pictures of my favourite bands that are in the centre pages and when they give you free posters.

Adult writing using an informal spoken style

I don't read newspapers very often. When I do, the sections that I read first are the bits on sport and TV. Most of the time, I hear the news on the radio or see it on TV so there's not much point in reading the same stuff in the newspaper. By the time it's in the paper anyhow it's old news. Anyway I'm not that interested in the news – it's all doom and gloom.

The writing in the first box is clearly that of a child – content and strings of ideas linked with 'and' indicate that this is the case. The text in the second box is written in a style that reflects how the writer would speak and, although it's informal, it's clearly the product of an adult rather than a child because it obeys many of the rules of sentence-making. It also expresses ideas in a more sophisticated way than might be expected from a child. Nevertheless, the adult text is highly personalized and uses connectors (such as 'so') that are more likely to be spoken than written. The writer uses vocabulary that is informal ('stuff') and idiomatic ('doom and gloom'). The use of contractions reinforces the sense that the informality of spoken language is being used to convey ideas.

Adult writing in a more formal style

Some people appear to have little interest in the news as it is presented to them in newspapers. Evidence suggests that sports and television features attract attention. However, there is a perception that newspaper items are superseded by television and radio broadcasts. This may also be the case for websites. One criticism of news items is that they tend to focus on depressing topics.

This final example, which is written rather than spoken, conveys its information in a neutral 'voice' by using generic terms ('Some people', 'evidence suggests', 'there is', 'one criticism . . . is') and by using passive constructions ('it is presented', 'are superseded'). The ideas are linked by connectors ('however'). Another feature of the type of writing that is reporting opinions, evidence or perceptible trends is that it uses language that 'hedges' ('appear', 'suggests', 'perception that', 'may also', 'tend to'). It's a style used in academic discourse when the writer's exploring a variety of aspects of a topic and doesn't want to give the impression that he's favouring one view over another.

Different formats for academic writing – possible elements

COMMON STYLISTIC FEATURES	⇒ uncomplicated sentences using technical language but avoiding jargon/cliché				
	⇒ clarity → relevance → reality → honesty				
	⇒ monitor use of passive ... is it necessary? Could it be said more simply in the active?				
COMMON FEATURES	*Titles*	*Numbered pages*	*Footnotes*	*References or Bibliography*	*Appendices*

LENGTH of TEXT

(Diagonal arrow showing increasing length of text, with categories:)
NOTES → ESSAY AND EXAM ANSWERS → PROJECT PRESENTATION LABORATORY REPORTS → REPORT → DISSERTATION → THESIS → BOOK

In accordance with preferred style. For personal use and non-assessed

	NOTES	PROJECT PRESENTATION LABORATORY REPORTS	REPORT	DISSERTATION	BOOK
	Suggested Format ↓	Suggested Format ↓	Suggested Format ↓	Suggested Format ↓	Format ↓
	1. INTRODUCTION	Title	Title page	Title	Contents
	1.1 Outline problem	Abstract	Abstract	Abstract	Preface
	1.2 Outline main points of answer	Author	Contents	Declaration	Chapters
	2. MAIN BODY	Date	Introduction	Acknowledgements	Bibliography
	Format dictated by key question word	Aims	Main body of the report	Contents	Index
	3. CONCLUSION	Literature review if applicable	Conclusions	Introduction	
	3.1 Summary of main points	Hypothesis	Recommendations	Literature Review	
	4. REFERENCES	Materials and methods	Appendices	Method	
		Results	Glossary	Discussion	
		Discussion	References	Conclusions	
		Conclusion	Index	Appendices	
		Recommendation	Illustrations	Glossary	
				References	
Assessment:		*Internal Marker and External Examiners*	*Internal and External Examiners*	*Internal and External Examiners*	*Peer review*
Presentation:		• *Personalized style*	• *Rigid parameters*	• *Rigid format*	• *Publishing house style*
Length:		• *Several pages* • *Word limit often imposed*	• *Chapter divisions*	• *Refer to regulations*	• *Publisher prescribes*

Exam essays

Another form of academic writing is that required for exam essays and they sometimes induce anxiety, even panic. But, in terms of style, conventions and purpose, the requirements are still the same as for other essays you've written; arguments still have to be supported, evidence presented and so on. The difference, of course, is that you don't have access to libraries and notes, and the pressure of time is acute. Nonetheless, we think that the techniques we've been describing throughout the book can still help you to organize and present your material clearly and effectively:

- So, once again, take it step by step.

- Before you go in, you'll know how long the exam will last and how many essays you're expected to complete, so work out a timetable, giving an equal amount to each essay and, within each essay, an appropriate amount to:
    - understanding the question
    - brainstorming
    - structuring
    - writing
    - editing.

- Read the questions carefully, mark the ones you feel most confident about and, from that list, choose the ones you'll answer.

- Allocate time to each, then forget about everything except the one you're writing first. That can be your 'best' one or the 'weakest', it's up to you.

- Identify the instruction words and work out what is the main topic, the particular aspect or aspects of it you need to focus on and any restricting elements contained in the question.[1]

- Now do some brainstorming. Jot down all your ideas as they come, follow every avenue that you open, get as much down on the page as possible. And, when you've done that, use the technique of looking at them one by one and putting them into categories as we did in our RED, BLUE, GREEN, etc. example in Chapter 4.

---

1 See Ch. 1, pp. 7–9, to remind yourself of what we mean by aspects and elements.

- Put the notes in each category in order, then organize the sequence of categories.

- And that's it. You've got your essay plan.

- The next step is either to write it, by linking the individual notes, and then move on to the next essay, or put it aside and prepare the plans of each of the other essays in turn. If you take the second course of action, you'll have your plans all ready so, if you start running out of time, you can quickly sketch an answer for the last one.

- But try not to run out of time. Stick to the timetable you've set yourself. If you start giving extra minutes to one question, it might earn you a few more marks but the likelihood is that you'll then have to rush one of the other answers and you'll lose more than you've gained.

- Leave time at the end to edit your essays. Read them carefully as the editor, not the writer.

If you fix this technique in your mind before you go into the exam, it'll help you to overcome the natural tension that exams can generate.

Instruction words

In assignments, you're usually asked to do one (or more) of three things: describe, analyze or argue. Different disciplines call for other procedures, such as calculations, but there's always at least one instruction word for you to follow. We've selected some of the more common ones, listed them opposite, and given an indication of what they mean. We've also added four columns on the right to cover the main three categories of instruction and another, more general one. It'll help you to understand and fix the meaning of the various instructions if you tick what you think is the most appropriate column for each word.

Instruction	Definition	Describe	Analyse	Argue	Do
Account for	Give reasons for				
Analyse	Look in detail at the topic, considering all its aspects				
Apply	Put a theory into practice				
Assess	Decide on the value or importance of				
Comment on	Give your opinion of				
Compare with	Discuss similarities; draw conclusions on common areas				
Compile	Make up (a list/plan/outline)				
Consider	Describe/give your views on a subject				
Contrast	Discuss differences				
Criticize	Point out weak and strong points in a balanced answer				
Demonstrate	Show by examples/evidence				
Describe	Explain process, appearance, operation or sequence				
Devise	Make up				
Discuss	Give your own thoughts + support your opinion				
Evaluate	Decide on the merit of situation/argument				
Exemplify	Show, by giving examples				
Expand	Give more information				
Explain	Give reason for – say why				
Explain how	Describe how something works				
Give an account of	Describe				
Identify	Pinpoint/list				
Illustrate	Give examples				
Indicate	Consider how something arises but not in great detail				
Justify	Support the argument for . . .				
Outline	Describe basic factors – limited information				
Plan	Think about how to organize something				
Report	Make an account of a process, an event				
Review	Write a report – give facts and views on facts				
Show	Demonstrate with supporting evidence				
Specify	Give details of something				
State	Give a clear account of . . .				
Summarize	Give a brief account of . . .				
Trace	Give a brief chronology of events or process				
Work out	Find a solution, e.g. as in a maths problem				

Note-making and note-taking

Although these terms sound broadly similar, the difference isn't just one of terminology.

Note-making is what you do yourself when you decide that you want to keep a record of what you've read in a printed source, for example, books, journals, newspapers, professional or primary documents such as Company Reports, contracts or Acts of Parliament. In this instance, how you take the notes is essentially up to you, although it may be influenced by the content and style of the source material you're reading. The point is that you can scan the whole text and then make decisions as to which note-making technique you'll use.

Note-taking is what you may have to do in a lecture, a tutorial, a course/group meeting or seminar presentation, which means that you won't have the advantage of being able to check the material before you make your decision. The notes you take and the style you adopt will be dictated by the content and also by the media the person or people whose ideas you're wishing to jot down are using. So you probably won't know what the line of thinking will be and you'll have to make an on-the-spot decision about how you're going to keep a record of it all.

In both cases, there are some fundamental things that you can do to make sure that the information is retrievable and reusable either for writing or revision purposes.

'House-keeping' tips. Note the following:

Note-making	Note-taking
• source, i.e. author name and initial, date of publication, title of resource, place of publication and publisher	• name of presenter, topic of presentation and location
• where you obtained the resource, e.g. library, Internet, own textbook	• date of presentation
• date that you made the notes	• page numbers of your own notes
• page numbers consulted	

Things to take down in your notes

- Titles, dates and authors of important references, publications
- Names of important contributors in the field
- Key terms explained in the text or lecture (cross-referenced with any glossary available)
- Analytical sequences of arguments, discussion, alternative viewpoints
- Examples of points to illustrate key issues
- Sources of quotations
- Figures/data to support line of argument or sequence of mathematical working.

Things to note in the margin/separately, e.g. by using a different colour of pen

- Things to look up later
- Reference details, e.g. Kirton and McMillan, 2006
- Your own view on the point(s) alongside
- Questions that occur to you as you read or listen.

Of course, notes are relatively worthless if they're not legible or if you never look at them afterwards. It all turns into a mechanical exercise and it means you've wasted time and effort on them. However, if you consider HOW you create notes, whether from listening or reading, you realize that they give you a potential source of information to use when you're thinking about your writing topic.

A good starting point is to be aware of the structure of what you're reading or hearing as this can guide your written record in note form. In the table below, we show how different approaches to a topic or issue are used in lectures and we suggest ways that might be good responses to these different functions.

Approaches to a topic

• Description, e.g. a sequence of events, an outline of a process	• Flow chart • Time-line • Numerical list
• Themes, e.g. short-medium-long-term; economic, social, political	• Keywords • Idea clusters/maps
• Analysis, e.g. looking at an issue from a variety of angles	• Idea clusters/maps • Matrix notes
• Dichotomies, e.g. looking at results achieved under controlled/experimental conditions; cause/effect; positive/negative	• Matrix notes • Either/or column notes
• Evaluations, e.g. problem-solving issues	• Situation – problem – evaluation – solution – recommendation sub-headings.

Example 1: Flow chart – harnessing sources of power

Here we offer eight different approaches to note-making and note-taking. The method you choose will depend on the aspect of the subject being covered and on your purpose in recording the notes.

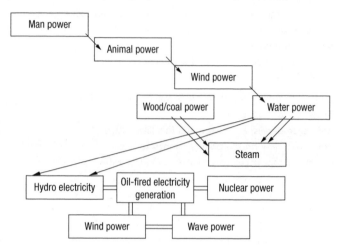

Example 2: Time line – development of the WWW

1837	Telegraph invented and patented
1858–66	Telephone invented
1957	First sputnik launched and beginning of global communication
1962–68	Military technology used to send information electronically in packets
1969	Birth of the Internet
1971	Email invented
1973	Global networking developed
1977	Email fully developed globally
1983	Internet enlarges
1984	Number of Internet hosts hits 1,000; UK's Joint Academic Network (JANET) established.
1987	Commercialization potential of Internet recognized
1989	Internet hosts reach 100,000
1992	Internet hosts reach 1 million
1993	WWW revolution begins; 2 million hosts
2000	90 million hosts and 68 million websites
2005	1,030 million hosts, i.e. 18% of the world's population can access the Internet

Example 3: Numerical (linear) notes

Topic Preparing for examinations

I	I.I	Identify the number of topics you need to revise.
	1.2	Collect the relevant notes.
	1.3	Ensure that all notes are organized by topic and include lecture notes and supplementary notes.
2	2.I	Map out a timetable for the starting point of revision until the exam date, making sure that you have allocated time for eating, sleeping and other chores and commitments.
	2.2	Allocate a time in hours that you think you will need to cover this topic.
	2.3	Prioritize the topics according to your interest/confidence in your understanding.
	2.4	Map these onto your blank revision timetable.
3	3.I	Begin by reading over your notes highlighting key points if not already identified.
	3.2	Refine your notes by turning them over and trying to remember the key ideas, words or issues that relate to the topic.
	3.3	Check your accuracy with original notes.
	3.4	Turn over notes again and try to flesh out key word/issue with greater detail.

Example 4: Keyword notes – total knee replacement

Total knee replacement

Joint replacement (JR):	– greatest advance in arthritis treatment in last 30 years
	– new lease of life
	– avoids confinement to wheelchairs and related health problems
Total knee replacement (TKR)	– aids mobility
	– relatively cheap to implement
Process	– removes rough surfaces of bone joint
	– replace with smooth implant surfaces
	– need for great precision on part of surgeon to achieve a good fit
Materials	– some components metal, others plastic
	– assembled in process of operation
	– mixture of materials causes fewer problems than metal-metal components
Fixing materials	– cement fixing has 10–15 yrs of 'life' before loosening
	– other alternatives still under investigation
	– ...

Example 5: Idea cluster maps – use of the Internet[2]

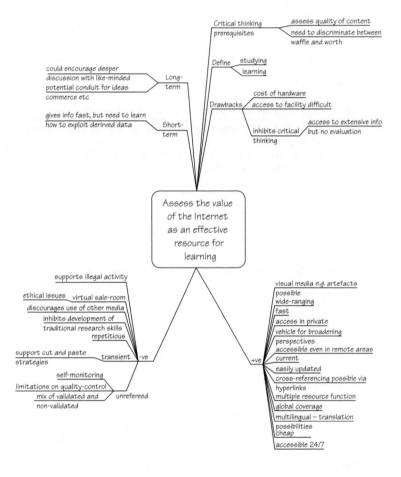

---

2 You'll find this same diagram in the QR on spider diagrams, etc., p. 162, with some explanatory text on p. 159.

Example 6: Matrix notes – problems of urban housing provision

Stakeholders/ Solutions	Planning officials	Architects	Local councillors	Potential residents
High rise residential accommodation	High density solution	Loss of community for function	Social problems and upkeep costs high	Anti-social and depressing; loss of community
Use of brown-field sites	Uses up eye-sore sites; has potential for high density housing	Potential for innovative design on limited space	Solves land usage problems; reduces infrastructure requirements	Positions could be central but can be marginal; less enthusiastic
Use of green-belt sites	Less desired as this erodes the natural amenity peripheral to urban areas	Good location with ability to be innovative in design	Contrary to spirit of conservation; politically unpopular	Preference of rustic environment but conscious of conservation issues
Renovation of existing properties	High cost of monitoring renovation	Innovative schemes with potential for the unusual; confined by limitations of existing building shell	Popular politically; re-cycling historical properties otherwise functionally defunct	Desirable, unique properties high in prestige value

Example 7: Either/or column notes

This style of note-making is a refinement of the matrix note-style in that it draws up elements of a two-sided analysis, *e.g.* for and against, cause and effect, reason and result.

Cause	Effect
1 Warm, dry summers	1.1 Evaporation of water in reservoirs 1.2 Introduction of water-saving measures, e.g. hose-pipe and car-washing bans
2 Dry winters	2.1 Water reserves not replenished 2.2 Summer begins with low groundwater 2.3 Algae 'bloom' on ponds 2.4 Fish die 2.5 Ponds dry up
3 Flash floods	3.1 Do not solve problem because, although these fill rivers and lakes, needs longer consistent rain to replenish groundwater

Example 8: Problem-solving notes

Situation	UK has many run-down buildings of considerable beauty and also historic value
Problem	Often in poor repair Expensive to maintain Owners burdened with maintenance costs and death duties Cannot afford upkeep
Solution(s)	1 Part ownership 2 Charitable status 3 Open to public and charge for entry 4 Demolish least viable and use proceeds to maintain those in better overall repair
Evaluation	1 Considerable legal difficulties when multiple stakeholders in the properties
	2 Charitable status takes initiative away from owners but avoids death duties
	3 High maintenance costs; insurance and disabled access issues for buildings without design features to allow modifications and which potentially damage the 'charm' of the building
	4 Requires consensus as to selection of buildings to be demolished; difficult to achieve and fraught with legal difficulty
Recommendation	Select charitable status and opening to public on fee-paying basis as this helps recoup costs and allows heritage sites to be preserved in the national interest

Punctuation

Whole books have been written on the subject of punctuation but here we're concentrating on points that seem to cause problems for many academic authors. They're listed in alphabetical order.

Apostrophes (')

Basically, apostrophes are a sign that something is missing. There are two main instances: when letters are left out to show ownership (*e.g.* the Queen's birthday) or when two words are contracted into one (*e.g.* is not = isn't).

Apostrophes showing possession:

In earlier centuries one way of indicating possession was to use expressions such as 'William, his book', which contracted to the form we use today, 'William's book'. The apostrophe denotes that the 'hi' has been dropped from 'his'. Of course, this 'rule' doesn't quite apply for 'Elizabeth, her book' where 'Elizabeth'r book' clearly didn't catch on. Thus, for male, female and inanimate or abstract objects, the apostrophe 's' became the standard. But, as usual, there are complications.

The position of the apostrophe showing possession depends on whether the owner is singular or plural. For singular owners, the construction is simple – you add 's to the singular noun (owner). *Lady Windermere's Fan,* Catherine's eyes, the student's essay. Of course, the 'possession' can extend to things other than people – the library's opening hours, the philosopher's theory, the government's hopes.

For plural nouns, the apostrophe often comes after the plural 's' – the students' essays have been marked (the essays of all the students); the Westminster politicians' constituents (the constituents of a number of politicians sitting in Westminster); the trees' leaves fall in autumn (leaves of all trees).

As we hinted, there are exceptions to this rule. Where a word takes a plural that's formed without simply adding a final 's', there's a slightly different arrangement. This involves only a few exceptions: children, men, women, people. Here the possession is shown by adding the apostrophe 's' because the words are already plural, so you get: children's toys; men's room; women's hospital; people's parliament. The apostrophe 's' also applies where a noun has the same singular and plural forms: sheep's wool.

If something is owned by more than one person, the second noun takes the apostrophe:

Tom and Jerry's antics are timeless in their comedy.

If there are several people who own different things, they all take apostrophes.

Students', teachers' and children's rights are distinct.

Apostrophes for contractions:
Language evolves and usage changes over time. This means that in speech people may have run two words into each other to form a unified word. In writing, this is shown as a contracted form that's more representative of the spoken language than the two single words ('there is' becomes 'there's'). This means that contracted words are seen as closer to spoken language and so seem to be less formal, and therefore less likely to be appropriate for academic writing.

Apostrophe confusion – its and it's:
Its – for possession.

The company took its name from its founders.

The brown bear lives off its body fat during hibernation.

It's – for contraction: it is = it's; it has = it's.

It's seven degrees below zero. It's been like this for eight days.

But note, no apostrophe is needed to show possession with any of the following: whose, theirs, ours, his or hers. However, it is needed to show possession for 'one'.

One's own decisions are often made impulsively.

Apostrophes do not 'make' plurals:
A mistake that often appears is the misuse of the apostrophe 's' to make words plural, for example potato's and tomato's which should correctly be spelt as potatoes and tomatoes in their plural forms.

British and American apostrophes:
The use of the apostrophe differs in these two systems in one respect, namely, when referring to decades when using numerals:

British style: the 1990s; American style: the 1990's.

Brackets ( )

Round brackets (. . .) – are used:

- to surround words that are used in a sentence to allow the author to make some aside.

  The Football World Cup (unlike any other sporting event) attracts record television viewing figures.

- and to surround figures in a list.

  Some consider that there are good reasons for retaining examinations as a form of assessment. This includes (1) testing students' knowledge (2) allowing students to show that they can work under time pressure, and (3) demonstrating how effective teaching has been.

Square brackets [. . .] – are used to surround words that have been added within a quotation, often in order to make the structure of the sentence complete.

'The religious integrity [of Henry VIII] was compromised by his decision to dispose of several of his wives in order to allow his later marriages.'

Capital letters (A, B, C . . .)

As with all forms of punctuation, capital letters are used to enable the reader to decode key information. Therefore, in English, initial capitals are used to name or introduce the following:

- 'I';
- Bullet point lists (such as this one);
- Countries (Britain), languages (Swedish), ethnic groupings (Celts), towns/cities (Paris) and the natives of these (Parisians);
- Days of the week, months of the year, festivals and holy days (but not seasons of the year);
- Historical periods, events or conditions (the Enlightenment, the Cultural Revolution, Stalinism, Postmodernism);
- Landmarks such as rivers (the Nile), mountain ranges (the Andes);
- Names of people and organizations (Alfred Nobel, the United Nations);
- Numerals at the beginning of sentences (Seven prisoners were found in the Bastille.);
- Peace treaties (Treaty of Westphalia, Treaty of Vienna);

- Religions and religious groupings (Hinduism/Hindus), holy personalities (the Pope, Saint Andrew, the Prophet Mohammed) and holy books (the Bible, the Torah, the Koran);
- Roles performed by specific personalities (Queen Elizabeth; President Roosevelt), but note 'The president of a company . . .';
- Sentences; and
- Titles of books, plays/films, poems, music, television programmes (*Treasure Island*, *The Mousetrap*, *The Lion King*, 'Ode to a Nightingale', 'Ashokan Farewell', 'A Question of Sport'), but note that in some referencing systems (*e.g.* the Harvard method) only the first letter of a title is capitalized.

Colon (:)

This punctuation symbol is used in four particular ways:

- to introduce a list such as this one
- to explain what's gone before

  Healthy eating requires a balanced diet: five items of fruit or vegetables per day, low fat content products and foods that contain only small amounts of sugar and salt.

- to give an example

  In international crises rapid aid is provided by non-governmental organizations: Oxfam, Save the Children, Médecins sans Frontières.

- to introduce a quotation

  The Justice Minister provided a definition of street crime: 'An act of deliberate violence involving the violation of another human being either by attacking physically, wounding or robbing.'

Comma (,)

Commas are the most commonly misunderstood form of punctuation – whether by omission or by over-use. Here are a few examples of correct usage.

Listing commas:

Red, amber and green are the colours used in traffic lights.

Between two adjectives describing the same noun:

The red, cascading blossoms are distinctive.

After connecting words, such as: consequently, furthermore, hence, however, moreover, nevertheless, therefore and thus. (See Quick Reference on 'Signpost' words.)

Joining commas – before and/but/or/yet/while:

- There are plenty of examples of misuse, plenty examples of overuse, and plenty of examples of omission:

  Moving home is usually an infrequent event, but it is stressful.

  We have the option of remaining where we are, or of taking the risk of escaping.

  Children may not enjoy reading for themselves, yet they are enraptured by good oral story-telling.

  Pedestrians regard the pavement as their exclusive right of way, while drivers consider the highway to be theirs.

For giving additional information about the phrase that precedes it (in apposition).

The Lord Mayor of London, Dick Whittington, had humble origins.

Alexander Graham Bell, the inventor of the telephone, was a Scot.

For defining.

Consider the following defining example:

Learners who are self-directed learn successfully.

The expression 'who are self-directed' defines the learners and is, therefore, an essential or defining part of the sentence.

Now consider this non-defining example:

Learners, who are self-directed, learn successfully.

In this case, the expression 'who are self-directed' is not an essential part of the sentence because it gives additional information. This becomes clearer if we change the expression to 'who are wearing blue socks'. This then gives some additional information about their clothing that does not relate in any way to their successful learning.

Common comma error

Using a comma between the subject of a sentence and the verb:

The botanist, monitored the intake of water in the sample plants.

This should be:

The botanist monitored the intake of water in the sample plants.

Dash (–)

This is longer than a hyphen and is used to add a further thought to a sentence. It's often used in informal letter-writing, but is infrequent in formal academic writing.

Diacritics (accents)

Diacritics are simply the marks that are used in some languages to alter the sound of a letter or letters, for example: señor; schön; élève; café; fête. The convention is to use the English translation of such words if they are known. However, in some disciplines, the use of a non-English word (and any diacritic) is deliberate as a means of identifying a particular condition, *e.g.* café society.

Ellipsis (. . .)

Ellipsis (three dots) indicates that the writer has omitted a word or words from a quotation.

Early symptoms of autism are difficult to detect . . . even for specialists.

Exclamation mark (!)

Generally, exclamation marks have no place in students' academic writing.

Full stop (.)

These are used to mark the end of sentences. Sometimes, they're also used to mark individual letters in abbreviations, as in *e.g./i.e.*

Hyphen (-)

The hyphen is immediately preceded and followed by a letter character, not by a space. It is used in the following ways:

- In double-barrelled names:

  The British Royal Family adopted the name Mountbatten-Windsor in the early twentieth century.

- In names of certain places:

  Weston-super-Mare

- In numbers (21–99) and in fractions:

  twenty-nine; three-quarters

- In different combinations to create a single word:

  Most students use loose-leaf pads. (adjective plus noun)

  Most students use note-pads. (noun plus noun)

  The well-known film actor, Sean Connery, is perceived to be the quintessential James Bond. (adjective plus adjective)

However, the status of the hyphen as a 'joining' symbol is erratic. Traditionalists would argue that words using a prefix should be hyphenated. Thus, post-modern, pre-historic, but usage and house-styles have dictated some disharmony (as you can see in this sentence). Therefore, the best 'rule' is to note the preferred format in your field, *e.g.* Postmodern as opposed to Post-modern, and use it consistently.

Inverted commas (see quotation marks)

Question mark (?)

The question mark is used instead of a full stop at the end of a sentence to mark a direct question, that is, the actual words of the question:

Do you plead guilty or not guilty?

A question mark is NOT used at the end of an indirect question:

The judge asked whether the defendant had anything to say.

Quotation marks (' ' / " ")

Single ('. . .') quotation marks are the preferred style for quotations in British English. Where there's a quotation within the quotation, then double (". . .") quotation marks are used. American English adopts the opposite format. The quotation marks surround the exact words that were spoken or written:

> Smyth (1997) favoured 'a new form of assessment where "student-centred learning" is the priority'. (British English)

> Smyth (1997) favored "a new form of assessment where 'student-centered learning' is the priority." (American English)[3]

Note that in the British English example, the full stop follows the final quotation mark because the quoted phrase is part of a longer sentence and not simply the quotation alone. In the American English format, the full stop is placed inside the quotation marks. Whichever convention you decide to follow, you need to be consistent.

Other uses of quotation marks (inverted commas):

For book titles:

> Most readers would find Tolstoy's 'War and Peace' a challenge.

For expressions that are particular to a specific academic community:

> The practice of bussing pupils to schools some distance from their homes was regarded as 'social engineering' of a kind that many considered inappropriate.

For expressions that the writer is presenting although not necessarily endorsing:

> The use of the tawse to 'discipline' pupils was a characteristic of Scottish education well into the twentieth century.

Semicolon (;)

The semicolon has three main uses:

- It performs a restricted task half way between a full stop and a comma. For example, if you need to link two short sentences without using a full stop, use a semicolon:

> People are wary of strangers; the unfamiliar is often perceived as a threat.

---

3 Note the (American) spelling of 'favored' and 'centered'.

- It's used to separate the things that are listed within a sentence where the items are not single words but quite long phrases:

    The conditions for rental of premises involve a number of undertakings on the part of the tenant including the prompt payment of the monthly rent; maintenance of the property in a clean condition; and use of the premises only for residential purposes.

- And it's sometimes used to separate points in a bulleted or numbered list. The penultimate point ends with a semicolon followed by the word 'and'. The final bullet is terminated by a full stop.

Slash (solidus) (/)

This mark is used:

- To separate alternatives:

    The fossil fuel/renewable energy source issue continues to be part of the anti-pollution debate.

    Every student must ensure that he/she has registered for the examination.

- To indicate 'per' in scientific writing:

    Sound travels at 331.4 m/sec.

- To indicate a period that bridges two years, as in an academic year:

    The year 1967/68 saw student unrest in many European cities.

Quotations and citations

Providing evidence is an important dimension of academic writing. You'll be able to do this by providing data from your own work but you may also want to show how your ideas or arguments are endorsed by citing the work of other authors, researchers or commentators. Citing simply means quoting ideas either directly or indirectly from other sources. It's particularly important for you to give your readers detailed information about the source of such material so that they can find it if they want to consult it themselves. A secondary issue, but one that's just as important, is that if you don't provide this information, you're plagiarizing someone else's intellectual property. As we've said elsewhere, universities have very strict rules about plagiarism and they'll penalize anyone who's guilty of what, in essence, is academic theft. So, to make sure that you don't risk falling into that trap, you've got to learn the conventions of layout and format that govern how to cite the work of others.

The most straightforward referencing system is probably what's known as the Harvard method.[4] Here are some examples of how it's used.

A direct quotation is included as part of the written text. If it's short, put it inside single inverted commas and don't separate it in any other way from your own words:

> McMillan (2006: 58) claims that individuals' personal circumstances are 'shaped by events in other parts of the "global village" where technology breaks down barriers of knowledge, communication, time and distance'.

If it's a long quotation, say thirty words or more, separate it from your own text (some authorities suggest using a colon, others favour no punctuation, but it depends on the format of the previous 'lead-in' sentence). To position your quote, type it in single line spacing and indent it on both sides. Add the author's surname, the date of publication and the page number below it:

> Human rights legislation is a fundamental of international law and has been the underpinning concept of post-war international organizations:
>
> > In the interests of freedom of expression, freedom of movement and freedom of the individual, there have been significant moves to protect individual freedoms since the war and these have been safeguarded in the Charters of the United Nations and the Council of Europe.
> > McMillan, 2006:57
>
> These principles, together with unfolding world events, ought to have harnessed the attention of the international community to global observance of fundamentals of liberty and equality.

But you may not always be able or want to quote extensively from other sources using direct quotations. For one thing, an assignment that's simply a string of quotations is still plagiarism, even where these have been attributed to the source. Depending too much (sometimes

---

4 See QR, Bibliographies and reference lists, pp. 130–2.

even exclusively) on the words and ideas of others is a type of plagiarism that shows a limited ability to think critically about the source material. So it's better to express the key idea that supports your discussion by summarizing what the source material says. You can do this in two ways. The first is the information-prominent style, when the author's surname and date of the publication, all in round brackets, come at the end of the summarized section, for example:

> It has frequently been suggested that international organizations provide little security for those whose interests they seek to further. However, this is regarded as a sweeping generalization that fails to identify the huge array of non-governmental bodies that contribute significantly to humanitarian causes, not just in times of crises, but in the longer term (McMillan, 1999).

The second is the author-prominent style, which includes the author's name within the sentence and the date of the publication is in round brackets, for example:

> McMillan (1999) holds the view that international organizations, while not without flaw, perform the function of maintaining lines of communication across political and geographical boundaries, often where governments have failed to do so.

Each time you use a quotation or citation, make sure that you put the publication details for all your sources in the template of your reference list. That way you won't miss out any references.

Frequently asked questions

How do I incorporate something that has been quoted in the original text in the section that I want to quote?

If there's a quotation within the quotation, the British custom is to use single inverted commas for the main quotation and double ones for the smaller one inside it, *e.g.*:

> Macbeth's guilt destroyed his peace of mind, causing him to cry 'Methought I heard a voice cry, "Sleep no more!" '.[5]

---

5 *Macbeth*, Act 2, sc. 2, l. 36.

What if I only want to quote a few words from a longer sentence?

If you deliberately miss out some words from the original, you must indicate the 'gap' by inserting three dots, a punctuation mark known as ellipsis, *e.g.* 'it is a tale . . . signifying nothing.'[6]

Let's invent a critic and a quotation from him. He's called Nottstead and, in an article on Macbeth published in 2001, he wrote 'the latest blood-drenched production left me wishing for the days when I could expect theatres to respect the Bard'. If we used it in an essay, we might say that Nottstead (2001) observed that 'the latest blood-drenched production left [him] wishing for the days when [he] could expect theatres to respect the Bard'.

If you are only providing a part of a sentence as a quotation, then ellipsis is used at the beginning and perhaps at the end of it, *e.g.*

> Nottstead (2001) wrote of a '. . . blood-drenched production . . .' and demanded that the Bard be shown more respect.

Can I avoid plagiarizing if I change one or two words in the original text and do I still need to give the author's name?

Sometimes, it might be better to make your point by putting a quotation into your own words but be careful with the technique you use because you can still be plagiarizing.

Take this example from another fictional critic called Holby who wrote in 1993:

> The formation of ideas in young children is frequently inhibited by the need to subject them to the formal requirements of educational theories. The need is to strike a balance between encouraging creative thinking and providing them with a secure grounding in the skills required to communicate with others.

Here's an example of how not to do it:

> Holby (1993) holds the view that the way young children form ideas is often adversely affected by the fact that teachers have to follow the formal requirements of educational theories. They should encourage them to think creatively and, at the same time, teach them the basic skills they need for communication.

---

6 *Macbeth*, Act 5, sc. 5, 1. 25.

All this does is keep a lot of the original and substitute some of the words. It's better to read it properly and summarize the essence of what's being said. A possible version is:

> According to Holby (1993), the imposition of educational theories at an early age stifles creative thinking and a more balanced approach is needed to preserve originality of thought while teaching basic communication skills.

Remember that, even though you've rewritten it, you must still say where it came from. If you don't, that's plagiarism again.

'Signpost' words

In writing, it's important to guide your reader through your text. You can do this by including some 'signpost' words to help the reader identify key points and trains of thought or argument. The following words are listed according to how they might be used. The functions are listed alphabetically. Note that *not* all of the markers listed here would be appropriate to both academic writing and spoken language. Those that might typically be spoken are underlined. (See pp. 160–1.)

Spider diagrams, idea clusters, brainstorming

Many people find that it helps their thought processes if they 'blitz' their ideas randomly on paper as a way of creating a visual representation of what they know. This can help identify connections, contradictions, advantages and disadvantages or emerging themes. It's a strategy that has been variously called brainstorming, mind-mapping, idea clustering and creating spider diagrams (a less detailed diagram). The figure on p. 162 gives an example of how such a diagram might be constructed for a topic on the use of the Internet.

Structuring arguments and counter-arguments

It's essential for you to be able to construct a strong argument either for or against a viewpoint. In taking up or refuting (rejecting) a position, approach or attitude, there are some fundamental skeletal structures you can follow. The examples on pp. 163–5, on the topic of home education, show you two ways of presenting and two ways of refuting an argument.

'Signpost' words

addition	• additionally	• either _ or	• neither _ nor
	• <u>again</u>	• equally,	• not only (X) but
	• also	• furthermore,	also (Y)
	• and	• in addition to	• or
	• and then,	• indeed,	• too,
	• as well as	• <u>in fact,</u>	• <u>what is more,</u>
	• besides (this)	• moreover,	

cause (reason)	• as	• due to	• in response to
	• as a result of	• for the reason that	• in that
	• because	• for	• since
	• because of	• inasmuch as	

comparisons	• by the same token	• in comparison with	• similarly
	• compared with	• in the same way	
	• in like manner	• likewise	

conditions	• even if	• on condition that	• unless
	• if	• only if	
	• given that	• providing that	

contrast and	• although	• in spite of (this)	• regardless (of this)
concession	• besides	• instead,	• still
	• but	• naturally,	• though,
	• by contrast,	• nevertheless,	• whereas
	• conversely,	• nonetheless,	• while
	• despite (this)	• notwithstanding	• yet,
	• even though	• <u>of course,</u>	
	• however,	• on the contrary,	
	• in contrast,	• on the other hand,	

effect (result)	• accordingly,	• for that reason	• the consequence is
	• as a result	• hence	that _ then
	• as a consequence	• so that	• therefore
	• because of	• so	• thus
	• consequently,	• so much so that	

examples	• as (evidence of)	• including	• particularly,
	• as an illustration,	• in particular,	• such as
	• especially,	• let us take (the case of)	• thus,
	• for example,	• <u>like</u>	• to demonstrate this
	• for instance,	• notably,	• to illustrate this

giving alternatives	• again • alternatively	• <u>better still</u> • on the other hand	• the alternative is
inference(s)	• if not • in (that) case	• otherwise • that implies	• then
numbering	• at first, • firstly, secondly, etc. • finally,	• initially, • in the first place, • last,	• next, • <u>to begin with,</u> • then,
reasons	• as • as a result of • because	• due to • in order that • in order to	• in response to • since • so as to • so that
results	• accordingly, • as a result, • consequently,	• for the reason that • hence, • the consequence is that	• then • therefore, • thus,
rephrasing	• <u>in other words,</u> • rather,	• <u>that is to say,</u> • <u>to put it more simply,</u>	• to paraphrase
summarizing / giving conclusion	• finally, • <u>eventually,</u> • hence, • in all	• in conclusion, • in short, • to sum up, • in brief,	• lastly, • to summarize • therefore, • thus, • to conclude,
time	• after (a while) • afterwards • at first • at last • at the same time	• before (that time) • eventually, • finally, • in the end, • meanwhile, • next	• previously, • since (then) • so far • subsequently, • then • (up to) then
transition	• as far as _ is concerned • as for	• incidentally, • <u>now</u>	• to turn to • with (reference) to

Spider diagrams, idea clusters, brainstorming

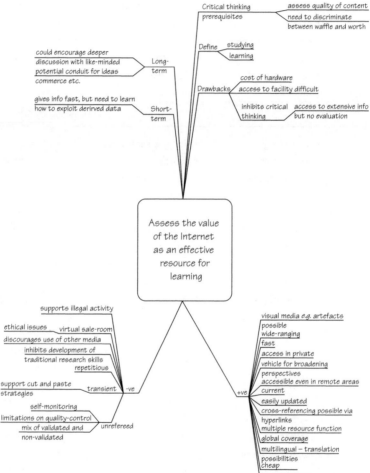

Presenting a written argument

Method 1

<u>In home education, teaching can be conducted within a familiar environment.</u>	Reason 1A
Teaching is usually done by a parent and this means that there is no need for learners to readjust to different teaching styles. <u>Parents</u>	Reason 2A
<u>can control the 'learning day' to fit in with the daily life of the family.</u> Another dimension of	Reason 3A
learning in the surroundings of the home is the potential for children to have exclusive use of all media available there. <u>Thus, the amenity</u>	Reason 4A
<u>of the home and the freedom to fit learning around family activities is an important asset in home education.</u>	Conclusion A

In terms of learning, in home education the child is being monitored closely across all subjects by the same person and the teaching materials can be selected to suit both the learning style and the interests of the child.	Reason 1B
<u>For children with siblings, they can also benefit from working alongside older and younger children in some respects.</u> At the	Reason 2B
same time, levels of work can be tailored appropriately to meet the needs of the individual child. <u>This suggests that there is</u>	Reason 3B
<u>much to commend home-schooling as providing a closer 'fit' to the development needs of children as individuals.</u>	Conclusion B
It seems, therefore, that there is a strong case for suggesting that it is better for children to be educated at home.	**MAIN CONCLUSION**

Presenting a written argument

Method 2

<u>There is a growing body of opinion that supports the view that it is better for children to be educated at home.</u> Teaching, usually done by a parent, can be conducted in the familiar environment of the home. <u>This means that there is no need for learners to adjust to different environments and different teaching styles.</u> Parents can control the 'learning day' to fit in with the daily life of the family. <u>In practical terms, children can have exclusive use of all learning media available in the home.</u>	<u>Main</u> <u>statement</u> Supporting statement A <u>Reason 1A</u> Reason 2A <u>Reason 1A</u>
The level of work can be tailored more appropriately to meet the needs of the child. <u>This is possible for two reasons: the child is being monitored closely across all subjects by the same person</u> and the teaching materials can be selected to suit both the learning style and the interests of the child. <u>For children with siblings, the learning environment can benefit from working alongside older and younger children.</u>	Supporting statement B <u>Reason 1B</u> Reason 2B <u>Reason 3B</u>
<u>It appears, therefore, that there is much to commend home-schooling from the viewpoint of the family and the child.</u>	<u>Restatement</u> <u>statement</u>

Refuting an argument in writing

Method 1

It is a commonly held view that home education is better than school-based education. This is the view held by the National Home Education Association, which claims to represent more than 2,000 home educators in the UK.	Reported opinion Reported support
However, this is not an idea that is universally accepted. Many argue that home-educated children fail to develop as well as school-educated youngsters. It is claimed that home-educated children are less well-adjusted socially, have access only to limited resources of indifferent quality and are taught by people not trained to teach.	Disagreement Support for disagreement Counterargument

Refuting an argument in writing

Method 2

Home education is not the best option to facilitate children's learning. There is a considerable body of opinion claiming that children educated at home are weak in social skills. This may be attributable to the fact that these children have only limited exposure to their peers and so do not develop these and other skills such as collaborative working.	Main statement Supporting statement 1 Reason 1.i Reason 1.ii
There is also a view that the standard of education cannot realistically be commensurate with that gained within mainstream schooling. It is argued that home education relies on limited resources and is being delivered by parents who do not have the appropriate knowledge or training to deliver the full curriculum.	Supporting statement 2 Reason 2.i Reason 2.ii

Using an index

For most of you, reading entire books isn't a realistic option, especially when you're trying to deepen and broaden your reading about a particular subject. However much you may want to read everything, there just isn't time, so it's important that, when you're reading to research a specific topic, you read selectively. In most textbooks, there are two ways you can do this. The first is to consult the contents pages. In most cases, the titles listed there indicate the general content of individual sections or chapters. The second area for accessing the finer detail of the content of a book is the index, because this enables you to pinpoint key words and topics.

Sometimes the index is divided into a general index and an author index. The author index allows you to find all references to particular authorities cited in the book. This is helpful when you want to track the approach or opinion of individual authors as described in the text. The general index provides the book's key topics and themes. A typical layout of a general index might look like this:

Example:

> Acculturation **18–23**
> Assimilation   **17–23**
> Bilingualism
>   – Ascendant 93, **100**
>   – Balanced 29, 45, 57, **102**
>   – Covert 30, **104**
>   – Subtractive **103**, 120
> Culture   19, 24, **16–30**, 29, 60.
> Education   100
> Ethnography   78, **86–9**

- Figures in bold indicate key or in-depth coverage, explanation or definition.
- Figures in standard text indicate that the topic is mentioned on these pages.

By selecting the 'in-depth' pages, you will be able to concentrate your reading on the most relevant content and avoid wasting time on passing references to your target topic.

Word-processing tips

These are some simple pieces of computing 'know-how' that might be useful in saving you time and frustration as you type up your work.

Spacing

- A single space follows most punctuation marks, but NOTE that apostrophes generally do not require a missed space. Some conventions require two character spaces between sentences, others prefer one. Whichever you choose, you should be consistent.

- For the first example in the text that follows, the typist has pressed the return key at the end of each line and this has resulted in an automatic (but incorrect) capital letter at the beginning of the new line. The second example shows that if you keep typing even when you reach the end of the line the computer will automatically place text on the next line if there's no more space and the intrusive capital letter is avoided. (This is called wrapping.)

  The conditions under which operations for total hip replacement take Place have been well documented in the literature but there is still Some considerable controversy about the positioning of the patient On the operating table.

  But with wrapping this automatically appears correctly:

  The conditions under which operations for total hip replacement take place have been well documented in the literature but there is still some considerable controversy about the positioning of the patient on the operating table.

- It's customary in the sciences and in engineering, but increasingly also in other areas of study, to use the left-hand margin as the beginning of paragraphs and then use the blocked style throughout. This means that there's no indentation for paragraphs, except for the opening paragraph of the text, which is indented. However, you then need a double line space between paragraphs.

Margins

If you use the justification function on the toolbar you'll end up with paragraphs that follow a straight edge down both right and left sides. This makes the text look neater and also prevents a 'ragged' look if the text is already being interrupted by diagrams and calculations.

Spell checker

Treat this facility with caution. Provided that you have typed a legitimate word, the checker will accept it. This can mean that where there are words of similar sound but different spelling you could find something ridiculous in your text:

* *The were 5 bear wires in the appliance.* This is accepted by the spellchecker.

Don't rely on the spell checker. Also read text carefully yourself – just to be sure that there are no glaring errors.

References

Bloom, B., 1956. *Taxonomy of Educational Objectives, Handbook 1: The Cognitive Domain.* New York: David McKay.

Carlyle, Thomas. 2001. *Sartor Resartus.* London: ElecBook Company. http://site.ebrary.com/lib/dundee/Doc?id=2001751

Orwell, George. 'Politics and the English Language. The New Republic' (24 June 1946). In D. Wickenden, ed., 1994. *The New Republic Reader: Eighty Years of Opinion and Debate.* New York: Basic Books.

Siegle, L., 2005. 'This Much I Know'. *The Observer* Magazine, 22 May 2005, p. 8.

Wardle, Irving, 1968. *New English Dramatists 12: Radio Plays.* Harmondsworth: Penguin Books.

Wittgenstein, L., 2006. *Tractatus Logico-Philosophicus.* Palo Alto, CA: Ebrary. http://site.ebrary.com/lib/dundee/Doc?id=10053796.

Index

Please note that page references to DIY tasks are in **bold** print; references to the QR section are in *italic* print; and references to charts or diagrams are underlined.

eBooks